W9-CSQ-696

WIND IN MY FACE

Autobiography of
Gladys Dawson Buroker,
Pioneer Pilot

GLADYS BUROKER with FRAN BAHR

Copyright @ 1997 by
Gladys Buroker
11498 Sandra Lee Dr.
Rathdrum, ID 83858

All Rights Reserved
Printed in the United States of America
Action Printers, Coeur d'Alene, Idaho

Contents

Chapter 1: Soloing

Chalk up another record for an unknown from the cross roads.
Gladys Dawson, 18 years old, who graduated recently from Ferndale High School and who is employed at a gasoline station, last week chalked up a flying instruction course believed to be the fastest record ever. "Making her first solo flight after five hours of tutoring is the fastest time made by any girl or woman pupil in the United States," Herb Buroker, instructor, declared.
The Bellingham, WA, Herald, September 28, 1932

"Ya know who that was, honey?" asked Lena, as she banged through the screen door into the gas station. "That's Herb Buroker, the pilot out at Tulip Field."

I had been pumping gas a few minutes before for the good lookin' older man when Lena, my boss, joined us, draping her ample curves across the hood of the car. Embarrassed, I finished washing his windows and hurried back inside.

"Not the pilot!" I cried, slumping into a chair. How could I have missed my chance. The next time Buroker came by, I was ready.

"How much you charge for lessons?" I asked. His eyes glanced my way, but he and Lena went right on joking at the counter.

"I'm serious," I persisted. "How much do you charge?"

By the third time I was getting exasperated. "Look. I'm only seventeen, but I wanna fly!"

"Come on, Herb, give her a chance," said Lena.

"Okay," he said with a big grin, stretching his six foot two frame. "Since you're a friend of Lena's, I'll pick you up on my way out tomorrow."

It was June 29, 1932, when I climbed into the back cockpit of Herb's Waco 10. Herb checked the oil, gave me a cushion to boost up my 5'2" frame, fastened my seat belt, and handed me a helmet. Tubes that attached at ear level formed a "Y" under my chin and ran under the seat into the front cockpit. Watching him fiddle with the controls, I wondered what he was like.

The ride to Tulip Field had been a lesson. Herb, unlike Dad, seemed happy-go-lucky. Eighteen years my senior, he had no trouble filling the silence with jokes and questions and flying stories I only half believed. The thought that all men might not be bad slid through my mind, but I ejected it just as quickly. I know about men, I thought.

I swore I'd leave home after what Dad did to my pony the year before. Every Sunday afternoon I rode my little cayuse to Tulip Field, only eight miles from our farm. Snip foraged in the high grass while I locked my eyes on a bi-plane that soared and looped overhead. It took six months before I saved the money for my first plane ride and less than six seconds in the air before I knew I'd fly again. But all that ended when Dad lost his temper one day.

"Nothing's stayin' on this damn place that can't earn its keep," he snapped. Then he harnessed Snip to a plow. Not built to be a work horse, she balked at the weight, so he grabbed a leather strap and whipped her until she dropped. Then with both in full lather, he tore the harness off her back and chased her out the gate. Sick with grief and anger, I began plotting my escape.

The week after high school graduation, Dad had me hauling fire logs with our old work horse. On one trip from the meadow to the house, my period started. I dropped Dan's reins and ran to the bathroom to take care of myself. When I returned, Dad waited by Dan, his face twisted, his fists in knots. "God damn you, Gladys. If you can't earn your keep, you can damn well get out!"

Our eyes locked for a long, long moment. Then in silence, I dropped the reins and walked back to the house. Packing what clothes my small suitcase would hold, I hurried to the kitchen where Mom was washing breakfast dishes. "Good-bye," I told her quickly, giving her a little squeeze. "I'll be in touch." Then out the door. To where? I didn't know but I'd never be back. Dad had beat, controlled and belittled me for seventeen years; I decided then and there to do exactly as I pleased. Flying was first on my list.

"Hold the stick back while I prop the plane," Herb said, startling me from my thoughts. The engine caught on his first swing. He climbed in the front cockpit and put on his head gear attached to the umbilical cord running to my helmet. With it, Herb could talk to me, but I couldn't talk back.

"Okay, we're ready," he said. "Keep your feet on the rudder, left hand on the throttle, right hand on the stick." I felt him nudge the throttle forward as we taxied to the end of the field. Then he shoved hard, and we swung around, heading down the runway. I tried with all my concentration to feel what he was doing. The tail came up and the rudder moved. Suddenly we were airborne.

"Okay," he said, once we quit climbing. "Now use your rudder and stick to make a right turn. Now left. Right again. Hold your altitude." Oh no. I completely forgot to look at the instrument panel. With eyes glued to the altimeter and my hand moving the stick forward and back, I tried to follow his directions, but the plane handled like a boat in rough waves.

OX5 WACO 10, in farmers field they called Tulip Field, located between Bellingham and Ferndale, WA - 1931.

It couldn't have been five minutes before Herb said, "Time to head back. I'll take over." Even now I can feel the unexpected dive, my head nearly hitting my knees as we pulled up into a deep loop, forcing the breath from my lungs and my small frame deep into the seat. "Is this supposed to be fun?" I thought. The next thing I knew we flipped into a slow roll at which point my stomach reacted violently. It took every bit of strength left to hoist my head over the side.

Herb spoke into the tubes matter-of-factly. "Okay, we're coming in. Follow through on the landing." He must have been kidding. After we taxied to a stop, Herb climbed out and began talking with a friend. Drenched with sweat, I struggled from the cockpit to search for a rag to clean the side of the plane. I wasn't about to admit getting sick.

As my fifteen minute lessons began to stockpile that summer, I became more fascinated with Herb. Trained as a Navy aircraft mechanic during WWI, he came home with the flying bug. Herb quickly found his brief stints as mechanic, cat driver and life insurance salesman could never match the thrill of aviation. After soloing with Tex Rankin, owner of a flight school in Portland, Oregon Herb designed and built a parachute as a gimmick to draw customers to Tex's airfield. The chute folded neatly into a canvas bag. A metal ring attached to the bottom of the bag with one end of a 12-foot-long rope tied to the ring and the other fastened to the airplane. Theoretically, the jumper wearing the harness had only to step off the wing, fall 12 feet, and the chute would pull out the bag and open. Herb tested his masterpiece by attaching a sack of grain to the harness and shoving it off the wing of a Waco 10. It opened so smoothly Herb harnessed up and jumped.

Not long after, Herb hired on as a pilot/mechanic for Sound Air Transport Co. at Tulip Field, halfway between Bellingham and Ferndale, Washington—the same Tulip Field I haunted on Sundays. When the Depression hit in 1931, Herb bought-out his boss and continued a one man operation. To supplement his

Gladys soloed OX5 WACO 10. Tulip Field, Ferndale, WA - September 24, 1932.

income, he taught mechanics at Whatcom and Fairhaven High Schools in Bellingham, giving flight lessons after school and on weekends to the few who had money to burn or a burning desire to fly.

I fit the second category. After my first lessons where I learned the basics, Herb scheduled me for take-offs and landings on late afternoons when the air was calm. One day just as I thought how easy this seemed, Herb said, "Stop at the shed." Climbing out, he told me, "It's yours. Make three landings."

My mouth felt stuffed with cotton. I couldn't smile, much less reply. Taxiing to the end of the runway, I swung around and pushed forward on the stick. The tail lifted too fast, shooting me up like a paper airplane to 550 feet. As I banked right, I realized why—the plane weighed 170 pounds less than on the last takeoff. No longer tense, I pushed the nose down and throttled back a little. This was no time for the jitters.

My first landing went smoothly. I resisted the urge to jump out and start yelling, for I feared Herb might not let me make the other two. I bounced a little on the second, smoothed out the last and taxied back to the shed.

Herb waited with a bear hug and a long kiss for his first female soloist. Taken by surprise, I felt my knees turn to rubber and a blush sweep my body. Lena, standing next to Herb, offered a welcome distraction. "Gladys," she told me, her face shining, "you deserve this more than anyone I know," presenting me with a beautiful gold watch.

"Thanks," I stammered, looking up. At that moment a flash blinded me—a *Bellingham Herald* reporter was shooting pictures. That day I felt like a movie star, about to bubble over like the home brew in Lena's bathtub.

Chapter 2: Hangar Flying

"Can't I help?" I asked Herb as I watched him rebuilding a Waco 10 for a Bellingham airport owner.

"Sure," he said, with no hesitation. "Go sand the rust off the fuselage longerons."

While I was in training for my license the year following my solo flight, I wanted to learn everything I could. I expected hangar work to be dirty and hard. What I didn't expect was Herb's quiet chuckles to bounce off the Waco's wings and into my heart.

It started simply enough. Sanding the longerons was tough, but I was determined to show Herb I could do it. He must have been satisfied, for he soon graduated me to building ribs for the wings, setting up a jig to lock the rib pieces in place and then glue and nail the gussets to them. Before long I started feeling like a partner.

As I finished each rib, Herb attached it to a front and rear spar, the main support for the wing. While I worked, he primed the fuselage tubing and began connecting the fittings and control cables. Finally, when the wings were ready to cover, he looked at me with that now-familiar gleam in his eyes.

"How'd you like to make the envelope?" he said. Men considered any job requiring a needle to be women's work. Herb was no exception. He could sew if he had to, but why bother when he had such a willing assistant? He showed me how to cut the four lengths of 42" Grade A cotton fabric by measuring around the wing and back to the trailing edge. Then we piled the fabric into his Chevy coup and headed to his little house on Montana Street where I first learned to use a Singer treadle machine, pumping with my feet as the flat felled seams rolled out in front of me. By the time I finished, my legs were well-warmed for the eight block walk home. Herb had long since deserted me for the field.

Now came the step that required we spend long hours together. Herb picked me up at Lena's and filled me in on the

Tulip Field, Ferndale, WA - July 4, 1932.

details as we sped toward Tulip Field. He would run two ropes over the rafters in the shed and down under the leading edge of the wing, so we could lift the wing off the floor into a more comfortable working position.

With the wing in place, Herb slipped on the envelopes and reinforced the fabric along both sides of the ribs with tape. Next he marked the fabric to make sure our stitches would stay straight and equal. On the first four or five feet from the butt where the wing joined the fuselage, we'd have to place them closer together because of the stress from the prop.

I knew the stitching took hours. Anxious to begin, I positioned myself at the top of the wing, watching as Herb threaded the most deadly looking instrument I'd ever seen, a 14" needle, trailing a long heavy cord. Herb's flying stories came fast, as his fingers nimbly tied the cord and slipped the needle through the fabric to me, stitch after stitch. He was well known among his cronies for his hangar flying skills. If only I could recall his words as clearly as I remember his laugh.

"Tell me about parachuting," I pleaded with him as we sewed. I wanted the thrill of jumping into thin air almost as much as my pilot's license.

"It's dangerous-that's what it is," he replied. "I've seen people die."

Herb's first summer at Tulip Field, they drew in field packing crowds to the parachute/flying exhibitions and penny-a-pound rides. If all went as planned, Herb explained, the jumps weren't particularly life-threatening. The chute they used had a large canopy that reduced the chance of injury on landing, provided Herb's calculations were on target. Of course, there were no scales, no practice sessions, no trial runs to test the wind. Jumpers just put on the harness, buckled the helmet under their chins, and climbed into the front seat, hoping their courage and the contents of their stomachs stayed with them when they dropped into 3000 feet of air.

Judy Kingsmore, sister to Tulips Field's exhibition jumper, gave the flying service a real scare one weekend. Herb was flying

Advertising – Plane Rides

a Ryan B-1, a four place cabin monoplane, powered by a nine-cylinder, air cooled, Wright J4B Whirlwind radial engine. Hot stuff in 1929. The door had been removed for ease in jumping.

As the crew approached the jump run, Dean's sister sat on the floor behind the front seat with her feet on the step ready to hang onto the sides of the door opening and step off when the time came. Herb probably made a mistake letting Dean fly as assistant. Over the years I've learned that activities involving risk and concentration go better with loved ones at home.

As Herb pulled into the stall, he said, "Jump." The girl froze. Dean yelled "jump" again. This time she did, but it was too late as the Ryan had started to drop. The chute, billowing out, caught in the tail wheel. Judy swung twenty feet below, helpless and invisible to both pilot and assistant.

What now? Like the engineer of a roller coaster, Herb banked steeply, swinging her into view. She appeared frightened but safe for the moment. Dean tried to control his panic as Herb headed for the bay to attempt a landing.

"Wait," Herb told Dean, changing his mind at the last minute. "Maybe we can free her instead." He sent Dean crawling through the fuselage to check out the situation. It looked to him as though the fabric were hooked. Herb knew if the girl opened her emergency chute, the thrust might pull the main chute free, but it could also create a tremendous drag on the airplane, pulling her in both directions, helpless to break free.

Herb met Dean's eyes with a forced calm. "I'm going to fly back over the field and make a steep turn. Lean out the door as far as you can and motion for her to pull her emergency ripcord." Dean nodded. As Herb completed the 180 turn, the girl's emergency chute popped open. For agonizing seconds the main chute held, then slipped free, dropping like a limp sack. Twelve minutes and one lifetime later, she landed safely in a farmer's field. This near-accident stuck in Herb's memory for years, even though he never saw Judy again.

A much worse episode, according to Herb, happened that fall. On October 21, 1929, Herb and his assistant, Gus, took up Ed Mills, a young bridegroom of four months. The Waco 10, an open-cockpit trainer used for aerobatics, was guaranteed to turn passengers green and scare novice parachutists out of their wits. Because the plane had no door, one was forced to step up on the seat, back out onto the wing and white-knuckle the fuselage until the pilot gave the jump signal. Those moments seemed like a lifetime...clutching, waiting, the gale force wind screaming through the wires.

I can imagine what went through Ed's mind on the wing that day. I've been there myself. But I can't imagine what happened next. He stepped onto the wing and waited as ordered. Gus assisted, holding the chute in its bag and waiting for Herb to pull into the stall. Then, with no warning, Ed grabbed the chute from Gus's arms and jumped, clutching it so tightly that the chute could not pull free.

Herb and Gus struggled to drag Ed back, Herb pulling with one hand and controlling the airplane with the other. Losing altitude by the second, he didn't dare add power for fear of snapping the rope. They actually began to pull Ed in when the canvas split, sending Ed in a suicide plunge to the earth.

"To this day I wonder what I could have done differently," Herb told me, the needle temporarily forgotten. "I don't want you talking any more about parachuting," he said, looking at me hard.

A bond grew between us that summer, even though we hardly noticed at first. I knew Herb had a girl friend and couldn't believe this tall, handsome pilot would be interested in a strong-willed farm girl like me. Herb's fun-loving nature began to ease my general distrust of men, all of whom I suspected were mean like Dad.

My earliest recollection of Dad's temper was when Mom and I came home from church one day to find ourselves locked out. The house, when we finally got in, was in shambles, every drawer from the kitchen to the bedroom dumped on the floor. Dad would be fine for a few weeks, and then something would set him off. The razor strap for us kids was just a mood swing away. I can't say I was afraid as much as hurt by his violence and icy indifference.

Herb just seemed so different! One beautiful summer weekend, when he invited me to go pub-hopping in Vancouver, B.C., I surprised myself by accepting. Herb was as natural on the dance floor as in the pilot's seat. To my relief, he didn't seem to notice that it took me half the evening to drink my first beer. Every Saturday night after that if we weren't with some of Herb's friends, we were at the grange in Mountain View, swinging to the tunes of "Dark Town Strutters Ball," "Alexander's Rag Time Band," "Old Shanty Town," "Margie," and "Peg o' My Heart."

That fall, Herb asked me to go hunting with him to Weiser Lake near a farm where I had picked raspberries as a kid. Surrounded by cattails and covered with lily pads, Weiser draws water fowl on their southern migration and also provides good cover for hunters hungry for wild duck. Of course I couldn't say no, even if a BB gun was the deadliest weapon I'd ever handled. Herb took a few minutes to instruct me on how to fire the 20 gauge, warning that I must hold the shotgun tightly against my shoulder. Then we rowed the boat to the south end where we could hide in the cattails and take aim as the ducks flew in.

About an hour and a half later, Herb spotted a flock of birds in the distance. Would they land near enough for me to shoot? Tense with excitement, I stood up, gun against my shoulder, and waited. "They're coming this way," Herb whispered. I sighted on a duck and squeezed the trigger. The next thing I knew, I was gulping ice-cold water. The gun's kick had blasted me into the lake. Herb laughed so much that day I don't see how he kept from falling in too. It was years before I held a shotgun again.

Prohibition offered Herb plenty more opportunities for amusement. His Chevy coup had what was called a turtleback which he loaded with tools, leaving the rear end dragging like a moonshiner's rig. Herb knew all the roads watched regularly by the border patrol. Quite often after the grange dance, he'd say, "I think I'll take the long way home through Lynden and Sumas tonight," and without fail a red light would soon start flashing behind us.

"How about opening that turtleback and letting me see what you got in there fella," a patrolman would order through the window.

"You want it open, do it yourself," Herb would reply.

After about ten minutes of heated conversation, ending with a patrolman threatening to call the state police, Herb would pull himself from the seat and saunter to the rear of the car. After much key fumbling, he'd finally open the trunk, and the officer would shine his flashlight down on a mess of greasy rags and tools. The patrolman would flush, Herb would cackle, and off we'd roar into the night with another hangar story for the guys.

One day we pulled into Tulip Field to find a strange airplane at the end of the runway. Herb said it belonged to Pete Benzell who needed a place to tie down for a couple of months while he worked in the area. A few weeks later at the Bungalow Barbecue, Herb commented between bites of his hamburger about Pete's unusual flying hours: "He takes off before the sun is up, heading north and comes cruising in from the south by early afternoon."

A few days later Herb asked Pete to pick him up some dope if he would be going to Seattle. Pete was glad to oblige, but when neither Pete nor the dope showed by nightfall, Herb discovered after a few calls that the Everett police had arrested Pete for smuggling Chinese laborers into the states from Canada. Herb still needed his dope and saw a perfect opportunity. He flew to Everett the next day, marched into the city jail, and demanded his dope or his money. Dope had a multitude of meanings, even then, but to a builder of cotton-skinned airplanes, it wasn't snorted, injected, or smoked. After the commotion died down, Herb got his money, bought his dope, and flew home with another story to make the rebuilding job go a little faster.

Dope came in a can like paint and looked like Karo Syrup. (It's still available for builders of authentic replicas.) After stretching the fabric over the frame and shrinking it with water, we brushed six coats onto the Waco, allowing drying time between applications. When first applied, the dope sags the cotton like an old tent after a hard rain, but as it dries, the fabric draws tight again and stiffer with each application. After the first coats, we doped two-inch, pink tape onto all the ribs from the trailing edge up around the leading edge and back to the trailing edge again.

A flight to Bungalow Barbecue for lunch in OX5 WACO 10. Ferndale, WA - 1932.

For a nicer finish we also taped the flat felled seams. When the Waco's fabric began to take on a tight glossy appearance, Herb mixed the last coat with silver powder to deflect the sun rays and preserve the fiber.

While I was helping Herb with the simpler tasks of restoring the Waco, we had an understanding. He knew how much I wanted a pilot's certificate and gave me every opportunity to build my hours. I was constructing ribs one sunny afternoon when he called from the back of the shed.

"Would you like to fly down to Elliott Merrills at Boeing Field and pick up some rib cord and tape? I wanna keep working here."

Would I! Herb knew I'd never flown beyond a five mile radius of the field, but if he thought I could fly solo to Seattle, I wasn't about to argue.

"But how will I navigate without familiar landmarks?" I asked.

He grinned and handed me a roadmap. I grabbed my sweater, old suede jacket, helmet, goggles and gloves and headed for the door before he could change his mind.

With the optimism of the young, I did my preflight check, made a clean takeoff over the telephone wires, banked and headed south. It wasn't long before the terrain started looking unfamiliar, and I reached under my leg for the road map. Anyone who has ever flown an open cockpit airplane is no doubt smiling about now. I couldn't open the road map with my sheepskin-lined gloves, so I discarded them immediately. Even so, I couldn't hold the map with the wind blasting through the front cockpit. Undaunted, I held the stick between my knees to free both hands. Still the vibration and wind made it impossible to read. Herb apparently decided I was ready for seat-of-the-pants flying. But how was I supposed to navigate by the seat-of-my-pants?

Feeling apprehensive, I climbed to 3,000 feet to get a better look. Visibility was perfect with Bellingham Bay shimmering to my right and Chuckanut Drive, my new road map, weaving below. Samish Lake shimmered over the hill to my left, and green fields jigsawed the landscape. As I followed my ribbon guide south across Skagit River, islands sprouted through the brilliant waters of Puget Sound. How hard it was to keep my eyes on a black strip of pavement when flying through paradise.

An hour later, my euphoria evaporated. Nothing looked familiar. "Relax, Gladys," I told myself. "You're following the only highway south. That smoke ahead must be the Everett mills.

"Seattle's next," I thought. I knew I'd find Boeing right behind city center. Within minutes Lake Washington appeared, then the runway. I circled and headed into the wind, feeling horribly alone—not even a bird in the sky. My stomach felt the way it did when I soloed.

Taking a deep breath, I began my landing. "Okay," I said aloud as if coaching someone else. "Head down wind on the east side at 700 feet. That's about right. Now ease the throttle back to idle." I glanced down and saw only four airplanes on the ground. Hoping no one I knew would witness what might be a sloppy landing, I forced myself to refocus. "Good glide, Gladys," Now roll into a left bank and line up with the runway into the wind. Looks about right to flare. Pull back on the stick...more...a little more...all the way to the stomach."

I could see Washington Aircraft in big letters on the building ahead as I taxied in like I'd done it a hundred times before. The salesman carried out my box of rib cord and tape and cinched it into the front cockpit while I dug in my pockets for a one dollar bill. "Could you pump me eight gallons of gas?" I asked the line man.

Moments later he propped my plane and held the left wing while I eased forward on the throttle to face in the right direction for take off. An old pro now, I let my ribbon map drift around my vision while I settled back for another sensory feast: snow on the Olympic peaks, afternoon sunrays spotlighting the land. In peaceful solitude I flew north, knowing a part of me would forever belong to the air.

It seemed only minutes before Tulip Field came into view. As I taxied to the hangar and shut down the engine, Herb ran out to meet me with a grin wrapped around his face.

Chapter 3: Barnstorming

Several months after my first flight to Boeing, I returned to visit Galvin Flying Service. I'd heard through the grapevine that owner, Jim Galvin, planned a barnstorming tour of Eastern Washington and needed a parachute jumper. From Herb's sidestepping the issue, I knew if I jumped, it would be over his dead body. Well, Herb couldn't stop me now. He had moved to Vancouver, B.C.

"Can I speak to Jim Galvin, please?" I asked the tall man at the desk who seemed all elbows and knees.

"I'm Jim," he responded. "What can I do for you?"

I know my pitch for the job took him by surprise. He stammered around a lot before he said, "We weren't lookin' for a girl."

"But don't you think a girl would draw crowds better than a man?" I insisted. He looked over my 5'2" frame and sort of rolled his eyes.

"Well, I'll talk it over with my partner. Come back later this afternoon."

I stopped back around 3:00. Jim said he would hire me if I'd make 20 jumps. "Just be ready to leave in two weeks."

I discovered later that shy, lanky Jim was a flying addict who barnstormed for a fix. Those free, open skies must have given "getting high" its reputation because barnstorming for most early flyers had nothing to do with dollars and cents. It was a natural high that I too wanted.

Heading home I thought about all that had changed since Herb and I hunted at Weiser Lake in 1932. The Depression hit the aviation industry hard, and few were able to hang on. When Herb finished rebuilding the Waco 10 the fall of '33, he gave up his lease on Tulip Field (which reverted back to a cow pasture), stored his Waco and Ryan, and went to work for Curley Evan's Stage Line in Vancouver.

Shortly before Herb left, I quit working for Lena for a better paying job at the Hamburger Express in Bellingham. The tips

MENU

Aristocrat Hamburger .... .10

Tuna Fish .... .10	Peanut Butter................... .10
Fried Egg .... .10	Cold Ham .... .10
Hot Dog .... .10	Fried Ham .... .15
Ham and Egg .... .20	Denver .... .25
Lettuce & Tomato .... .15	Cheese .... .10

Limburger .... .10

SPECIALS

Ham & Eggs	Bread-Butter-Coffee	.... .35
Bacon & Eggs	" " "	.... .35
Hamburger Steak	" " "	.... .30
Chili Con Carne	" " "	.... .10

SALADS

Lettuce & Tomato .... .15	Combination .... .15
Tuna Fish .... .15	Potato .... .10

BEVERAGES

Coffee or Milk .... .05	Tea .... .10
Malted Milk .... .15	Milk Shake .... .10

DRAUGHT and BOTTLED BEER

Pie per cut .... .10

We make our own hamburger daily.
It is not accumulated.

Hamburger Express Menu - 1933

Hamburger Express – Gladys' first waitress job - 1933.

and wages soon grew to the thirty five dollars I needed to buy an old four-cylinder Indian Ace motorcycle I had fallen in love with. It wasn't long after that I set my sights a good deal higher. Pop Place owned the Harley-Davidson dealership in Bellingham. I found myself driving out of my way daily to gawk at the window display. I loved my Indian but knew I needed a more practical machine. The Indian's engine lay horizontally, exposing the spark plugs to moisture. When it rained, my right knee would do aerobatics from the electrical jolts.

I mustered the courage one day to stop. Pop showed me the Model 45 which suited me best, offering to take the Indian in trade for fifty dollars and give me two years to pay the three hundred dollar balance. He even offered to hold the contract, so I wouldn't have to borrow from the bank. I took the Indian for one last ride and turned it over to Pop.

My first day off I sped to Vancouver to show Herb my prize. Of course, I took him for a ride. The dike road we took was

Gladys with her Indian Ace motorcycle.

unfamiliar to me, but even so, I had to show-off. Accelerating at full throttle, I decided to turn left, realizing too late that the road I'd chosen hooked at a 135 degree angle. Even with the floor boards scraping the pavement, I couldn't turn fast enough. Throwing up dust and rocks as the bike skidded out-of-control, we came to rest in a mass of blackberry brambles. As the dust settled, Herb and I picked ourselves up, groaning, trying to laugh, and looking like we'd just lost a fight with a tiger.

Unable to see Herb very often, I just itched for a new thrill. That's why I'd hit up Jim Galvin to be his parachuter. And now I had the job! On the way home from Boeing, I stopped at the Hamburger Express to give my notice.

Bill Wegley, my boss, couldn't believe his ears. "You're gonna do what?" he shouted. Knowing my stubborn streak, he calmed down after a minute. "Well, finish out the week. If you want your job back when you're done barnstorming, let me know. And BE CAREFUL!" After dropping by the Harley shop to settle

Gladys with her first Harley Davidson.

25

up with Pop, who agreed to postpone my payments until I returned, I headed home to gather my gear.

Had I known what I know now, I might have handled things differently. When I checked in two weeks later, Jim told me first thing that Eddie Brown, his parachute rigger, had a 28 foot Russell Lobe exhibition chute he could sell me for thirty bucks.

What a shock! I hadn't figured on expenses, just on all the money I would make. It was either hand over thirty dollars or go home. "Okay," I said, "but do I have to pay for anything else?"

"Nah," he replied, "long as you bring a sleeping bag and don't mind bunking under the Swallow." My bedtime companion for the next three months was an open cockpit, 1929 bi-plane, powered by a liquid-cooled Hispanna Suiza engine. She generated a lot of power for her weight and sheltered me at night as best she could.

We left Boeing Field late one Sunday morning, just as the fog lifted from the Cascades. Mt. Rainier, magnificent in her snowcap, loomed to the south. To the north I could see the Columbia River winding from Wenatchee to join the Snake and spill into the Puget Sound. Below us the stubble of harvested grain fields lay in perfect symmetry like an enormous checker board.

We planned to meet Jack Sturgis, our advance man, in Pasco. By the time we sighted town, he was to have picked out a suitable landing field, arranged for publicity in the local newspaper, and put advertising posters in the merchants' windows.

As we neared our destination, my stomach began to churn. In all our discussions, neither Jim nor Eddie had yet mentioned how to jump. The Civil Aeronautics Authority (CAA), not requiring training for parachuters, only asked that chutes be packed by a certified rigger. Our man, Eddie Brown, was a soft-spoken bachelor with an English cap hanging over his nose and a wad of tobacco bulging his cheek. Not much over five feet tall, he looked more like a jockey than the Northwest's best-known jumper and rigger.

After we landed and made connections with Jack, Eddie began to fit the chute harness to my body and attach the emergency chest pack. I hoped my Harley sweater, suede jacket, and peg-top breeches tucked into high-topped boots would protect me from the cold and whatever abrasions I might get as I hit ground..

"Get on the plane," Eddie instructed, "and see if you can maneuver in and out of the cockpit." No problem, even with the bundle on my back.

"Okay. Now, standing on the wing and hanging onto the cockpit, reach your right hand under your left arm and grab the ripcord." It was a stretch, but I could manage.

"Good!" he said. "Now when you jump, don't pull until you count off ten seconds. And remember. Have your legs together and your knees bent when you land." That was my full academic course in parachuting. There really didn't seem to be anything to it. Just back out, hang on, jump and bend knees. No need to be nervous.

The sun was beginning to cast shadows. Almost time. I walked to the plane for Jim's last instructions. A feeling of finality

Pilot Jim Galvin and parachute rigger Eddie Brown making an engine repair in the Hisso powered Swallow, Washtucna, WA - 1934.

settled over me as I stepped on the wing. I felt clumsy with my emergency chest pack hanging down to my knees.

As I struggled with my seat belt, Eddie propped the plane. With Jim in the pilot's seat, we bounced across the wheat stubble, picking up speed. Then we were off, past the dust of cars, circling ever higher like a red tailed hawk playing the currents. The altimeter climbed—1,000, 2,000 feet. With each circle my anticipation grew, sending shivers up my arms and gripping my stomach.

At 3,000 feet Jim told me when he wiggled the stick to climb onto the wing and jump at his command. I felt the signal. Pulling myself up onto the seat, I strained to back out, one foot at a time. The gear felt so bulky I was worried. What if I missed the reinforcement and stepped through the wing?

As I stood upright, a seventy knot wind slammed into my side, freezing my cheeks and stiffening my knuckle-grip on the cockpit frame.

"Can I reach the ripcord?" I asked myself, wanting to touch its reassuring length.

Tearing my right hand loose, I grabbed. To my horror, I couldn't reach it! I grabbed again and again. With each attempt, I could feel the plane climb more steeply and glimpse the bleachers filled with upturned faces.

"Climb back in the cockpit," I told myself, "before you get killed!" But the hell-bent-for-fire part of me took over.

"Don't be a coward," I thought. "How could you face those people down there?"

"Jump," Jim yelled. I stepped off the wing to my death, so I thought, still groping for the ripcord.

Once free of the plane and the wind, the ripcord dropped into my hand. But when I pulled, nothing happened. Three seconds later, the chute opened.

In an instant I shifted gears from panic to peace. The wind filled the chute, snapping my body to attention. Then it relaxed, and I floated as in a dream, no sound or falling sensation disturbing the magical spell. The earth moved gently toward me until that shattering two or three seconds when the ground came up fast. "Bend your knees and roll, Gladys!" I reminded myself in the nick of time. The impact knocked the breath from me, but I felt solid earth beneath my hands and knees. I was safe and absolutely hooked.

For what seemed like an eternity, I'd sleep under the Swallow, living entirely off bread and baloney (no butter) until I couldn't take the dirt any more. Then I'd rent a hotel room for a night to take a bath and do the laundry. From the beginning I wanted to send money home to Mom, but after the second month, I realized I'd be lucky to make enough to eat. I wanted so badly to have Mom think I was doing well that I traded in my twenty dollar gold piece, a graduation present from the Garlicks, for a twenty dollar bill to send home.

The first two jumps at Pasco and Kennewick I made seven dollars, pretty good pay for those days. As we hit smaller

Gladys with her exhibition parachute - 1934.

29

PARACHUTE JUMP

By Miss Gladys Dawson

OMAK (Airport)

Sunday Afternoon

October 28th   2:30 oclock

Passenger Hops, $1 Per Person

Pilot, Frank Kammer

Independent Print, Okanogan

communities, it was a different story. The guys barely took in enough money to pay for gas. From that time on I never made more than two dollars a jump.

Though the money was bad, my confidence soared after the first jump and the crowd's applause. After a few more excursions, I learned through trial and error how to execute the best jumps. An airplane on jump-run always heads into the wind. When free falling, I'd leave the plane facing the tail with the wind at my back, so I could see any obstructions in my path. When heading for an obstacle, I would expose more canopy area to the wind by pulling down on the forward risers, thus increasing forward momentum. On a lucky day I would be able to maneuver over the object while still above it.

On not-so-lucky-days I suffered a few mishaps. One weekend in Moscow, Idaho, I jumped twice, once on Saturday and once on Sunday. The Saturday jump posed no problem whatsoever as the wind had died in late afternoon and the chute collapsed easily when I hit ground. Not so on Sunday. Jim had scheduled the jump earlier, and a good breeze was blowing. About halfway down, I realized my hands would be full as I moved as fast horizontally as vertically in the direction of a plowed field.

"Good," I thought optimistically. "At least it'll be soft." Pulling on the riser to clear a fast-approaching fence, I locked my legs together for the landing. When I hit, the ground cushioned my fall, but the wind kept the chute inflated, dragging me on my stomach toward the foothills, my body plowing a nice furrow as I fought to collapse the canopy. Thank goodness, some observers in a car finally intercepted my path. But when I stood up, they burst into laughter. Dirt had packed into my britches so tightly that I looked pregnant and ready to deliver.

Another jump in Lind, WA, gave me a more serious scare. I had a wind of about 10 mph, not strong, but enough to keep me busy when floating toward hazards. I was headed directly toward a dirt road intersection with all four corners fenced. Knowing I would hit the first fence if I didn't do something, I applied just enough riser to clear it before hitting ground in the middle of the intersection. The wind drug me across the road before I could collapse the chute, slamming us both against the barbed wire fence. Standing up a little shakily, I thought "Thank goodness Herb didn't see this jump!"

Gladys, Pilot Frank Kammer and Eddie Brown before jump from Curtis Thrush - 1934.

These misadventures came infrequently, so I didn't think too much of them. Instead I spent my energy exploring on the few days I got off. We flew into Connell, WA, one day, and I noticed a brand new airway beacon sitting at the end of the field. In the early 1930's the CAA installed these for navigation every twenty five miles along flight lines.

I decided to walk over for a better look. The hundred foot tower had a small metal ladder running from my feet all the way to the top—to me an invitation to climb. Captivated by the idyllic view of a small town surrounded by rolling hills of golden wheat, I stopped my ascent to admire the scene. When I looked down, though, I became disoriented and nauseous. Almost paralyzed, I forced myself to back down slowly, one foot at a time, until at last I stepped onto solid ground. For some reason the sensation of height when connected to the ground felt entirely different than in an airplane or a chute.

My seventeenth and last jump took place in Kennewick, WA. I was floating about three hundred feet up when Jim, unaware of my presence, took off beneath me in the Swallow. As I entered his slip stream, the turbulence partially collapsed my chute.

I hit the ground hard, pain ripping through my right knee. My leg crumpled when I tried to stand, and my knee quickly swelled like a balloon. Some friends I met insisted I stay with them that night. I gladly accepted, soaking in a tub of water. By morning the pain had eased some.

Knowing I couldn't jump for a couple of weeks, I flew back to Seattle with a friend of Jim's. I was in some pain but oblivious to the seriousness of my injury. Leaving Kennewick with sunny, blue skies, we hadn't gone far when a cloud bank appeared at 4,200 feet. Frank started climbing, saying, "Let's go up and take a look."

A broken layer of stratocumulus cloud stretched like an ocean before us, so we flew on top, planning to drop down through a hole in the cloud cover at Seattle. We couldn't have been happier. The sun sat at our backs, the clouds sparkled, and Mt. Rainier poked through the cotton blanket like a giant telescope.

Parachute Jumper Demonstrates Here

Miss Gladys Dawson of Bellingham, the only woman parachute jumper in the Northwest, jumped from a plane in the field just back of the town water tank, Thursday noon. A crowd of school children and adults had gathered for the event. Miss Dawson was forced, by a strong wind, to the southeast and she came down on the cross road by the Coombs Ranch, one mile from town. She said she had to maneuver about considerably or else she said she would have come down on the barn. She landed in the road. Several cars followed along and Mr. and Mrs. Oscar Loeffelbein drove to the landing scene a second time and brought she and her assisting man back to the plane.

Miss Dawson learned to pilot a plane in 1932 in Bellingham but has only been jumping for a month. She flies on a student's permit. She is also a motorcyclist.

Jack Sturgis is the business manager of this enterprise and Thursday morning solicited contributions from the local business houses, also took contributions at the plane.

Eddie Brown, well known parachute jumper, who has made 196 jumps, is with the party.

Frank Kammer of Wenatchee is pilot of their plane which is a Curtis Thrush cabin plane. Mr. Kammer spent a number of hours this summer doing forest patrol work in the Wenatchee and Chelan districts, and over the Cascades as far north as the Canadian border.

Prosser, WA News, 1934

About thirty minutes after take-off, at 9,500 feet, I saw something ahead. Although our airspeed in the Curtis Thrush indicated 88 mph, we gained very slowly. Soon we could see the object clearly—a magnificent bald eagle, clipping along at least 85. Every few seconds it would swing its head 180 degrees to eye us, then redouble his efforts to stay in front, no doubt certain we would kill him. "No wonder we pilots give up love and money to fly," I thought. "Very few human beings will see anything to match this."

After about two weeks at home, I grew restless. The swelling in my knee had pretty much disappeared, and I could walk without too much trouble. One evening the phone rang, and Mom answered. "It's that Galvin guy, Gladys. Tell him you can't go."

When I reached the phone, Jim asked, "When ya comin' back, girl? If you wanna jump, we'll be in Okanogan this weekend." I told him I'd be there. A little apprehensive, I reminded Mom I still had a contract to uphold, even if I didn't want to. "Three more jumps, Mom, and I'll be home."

The fellows seemed glad to see me when I arrived in Okanogan. Actually, it was the only time they showed any concern at all. I had supper with them and was back in my room

Gladys - Curtis Thrush, 1934

when someone knocked on the door. I opened it, and there stood Herb. "Get your things," he said. "I'm taking you home."

An Airplane RIDE **FREE!**

See Moscow from the AIR!

A few minutes work is all it takes

Pilot Frank Kammer, inset, and his Curtiss Thrush that will carry you on a free ride for a few minutes' work. Pilot Kammer holds a transport pilot's license and has been flying since the World war.

Saturday and Sunday

HERE'S HOW TO WIN A RIDE . . . .

Just take a few minutes and get six one-month subscriptions to the NEWS-REVIEW, and we will give you an airplane ride FREE! Bring the names of the six subscribers to the office of the News-Review on Sixth street before 5 p. m. Saturday. You don't collect a cent, just get the names, and the carrier boy will collect at the end of the month. The ticket you will receive will be good either today or tomorrow.

OR

Get one one-year subscription to the News-Review by mail with payment in advance. Collect the $2 and bring it to the News-Review office before 5 p. m. this afternoon and get your ticket good for a ride today or tomorrow.

PARACHUTE JUMPS

Miss Gladys Dawson will jump from the airplane this afternoon at 4:30 p. m. or immediately following the Gonzaga-Idaho football game, and again tomorrow afternoon at 2:30. Miss Dawson is the only woman parachute jumper on the Pacific Coast.

SPECIAL TRIPS
Special trips will be made by Pilot Kammer to any point in the Northwest. Charges for the trip will be made on an hourly flying basis.

IF YOU WANT TO PAY
for your ride, that's O. K. But why not spend a few minutes and earn a ride FREE! Children will be taken over Moscow for $1 and adults may have the same ride for................$1.50

The Plane is located at the Ed Kitts farm 1 mile east of the CCC camp or ¼ mile south of Moscow cemetery.

Chapter 4: My First Airplane

Herb's mouth pressed in a grim line as we packed my bags. Although I seldom knew him to swear, I gathered his confrontation with Jim and Eddie was brief. "You goddamned sons-a-bitches," he told them. "Don't you ever ask Gladys to jump again."

Herb quickly piled me into the car and headed for home. As we wound through the Cascades toward Bellingham, I stole glances at Herb's strong profile, surprised and flattered by the strength of his feelings. Finally, I touched his arm. "Thanks for pulling me out of this one, Herb."

"Sure thing, kid," he answered.

Everything changed for me that day. Both Herb and I had dated other people when he was in Canada. Though I wasn't about to let him know, I would never again see anyone else— ever.

Herb felt the time was right to try running his own business, and he definitely wanted back into the U.S. With his two airplanes and a new lease on the Snohomish County Airport, he had an ideal setup. So did I.

Now I was riding to Everett every day off to fly and spend time with Herb and the gang. Herb checked me out in the Piper J2 Cub (just new on the market) that he was leasing from a friend. It was a perfect student plane since its engine consumed gas at the rate of 37 1/2 horses compared to 90 in older models.

When I wasn't flying, we'd have lunch and sometimes dinner. Herb and I kidded a lot about who cooked the best although I usually made meals for him when I was visiting. One day he began bragging about his cakes, and I just couldn't take any more.

"That's just talk," I said. "I know I can bake a better cake than you!" The bet was on.

We agreed to meet the next week for a bake-off. Careful not to let the gang know which cake belonged to whom, we invited friends to try a piece of each and choose the winner. I doubt if my Double Chocolate Dream or Herb's Oatmeal Raisin Dandy would have taken any prizes, but by the day's end not a crumb was left. The outcome...a draw. The gang knew better than to choose sides.

About this time I was offered a job at the Leopold Hotel Coffee Shop and Dining Room, renowned for both its hospitality and elaborate menu which attracted a prestigious clientele. Each day I put on my black dress with white pleated apron and lace tiara, never sure who I'd see. I served Clark Gable, more handsome in the flesh than on the screen; Jack Oakie, who made *Call of the Wild*; and even the beautiful, well-mannered Shirley Temple, only six at the time.

My most memorable customers, though, claimed neither fame nor fortune. I was working alone in the coffee shop one quiet afternoon when six, modestly dressed women came in chattering and sat at a corner table. To my horror, among them were Miss Curtain and Miss Fromkey, my grade school teachers.

Perhaps it was lack of attention at home that turned me into a grade-school ringleader. I sure engaged in plenty of deviltry. One day when I was eight years old, I climbed in the teachers' rest room and locked the doors from the inside, a pressing

Leopold Hotel Coffee Shop waitress crew. (Gladys sixth from right.)

problem, you could say, for the principal. Another prank I favored was lobbing spitballs at teachers. I became so skilled that I seldom got blamed for mine, only for the badly aimed ones other students shot. (Most teachers knew I was up to no-good, so suspected me for any wrongdoing.)

My worst grades were the fourth and fifth with Miss Curtain and Miss Fromkey. The palms of my hands were always red from whacks, and I spent plenty of time in the principal's office. One day I remember particularly well, I engineered a fight between two boys and later smacked Miss Fromkey in the behind with a heavy duty rubber band. That did it. She chased me around the classroom, yelling, "Stop right there young lady!" When she finally caught me, she nearly shook the clothes off my back.

I know I deliberately upset the teachers. Dad's treatment of Mom, along with our frequent whippings with the razor strap, put me in a constant state of anger. Whatever I felt seemed a bit relieved when I could fight someone or antagonize a teacher...that is, until eighth grade and Miss Benthine.

Every bit the spinster school marm, Miss Benthine dressed the part with her long red hair held neatly in place by combs and her lace collar clasped in a brooch. Try hard as I might, I couldn't make her mad. When I misbehaved, she would just say, "Gladys, you will spend your lunch hour in the classroom." By the end of the school year, I had confided my problems and my dreams. Alone in her presence, with no one to impress, I began to feel worthwhile.

She proved I meant a lot to her one spring day. I had planted a large flower garden at our home on Maplewood Drive, the main north-south highway to Canada. Thinking to make some spending money, I built a roadside stand and sold tulips and gladiolus to passersby. After listening to me chatter on and on about my project, Miss Benthine walked two miles from town one afternoon to see my handiwork. That was before Dad burned my bulbs. For some reason her interest changed me. I put away my boxing gloves and began working hard in school.

Now, eight years later, I was suddenly faced with my unfortunate past. Nervously I served Miss's Fromkey's and Curtin's lunches and rang up the bill. To my relief they didn't recognize me, even though they continued meeting weekly at the coffee shop.

One day, as I was serving them iced tea, Miss Fromkey grabbed my arm and said, "Aren't you Gladys Dawson?"

I turned beet red and mumbled, "Yes."

"We've been talking about you-thought you were Gladys-couldn't believe you turned out to be such a nice young lady."

I tried to be the polished waitress the Leopold management expected, but it did tax my patience. Dressing the part was hardest, a problem I had been facing for years. Mother tried hard to mold me into a lady, but feminine ways never did come naturally to me.

It seems odd, then, that Madeline Thompson, another waitress, became my life-long friend. Madeline loved dressing up as much as I hated it, never stepping out without makeup, jewelry, and perfect hairdo. But her bubbly personality and obstinate, little nose signalled a daring personality that matched mine, tit for tat. Madeline would go any place with me on the Harley and loved the out-of-doors. She also adored men and found plenty of prospects in the gang I hung out with.

Gladys' flower garden at age 14.

Shortly after we met, Madeline and I rode over to Pop's for a rally where we found several of my friends discussing a cross country tour. Madeline's eyes met mine, and we made a pact. "Let's do it!" she said. "Okay," I replied. Unfortunately, the trip was to be a year and a half in the making. We had money to save, and I needed a new bike.

Meanwhile, I continued socking away hours for my pilot's license at Snohomish County Airport. One day Herb said, "Come out in the shop. I have something to show you." In a box next to his vice sat a perfect, little engine.

"What's it for?" I asked.

"It's for that motorcycle you want to build for your kid brother," he answered.

I was elated. Ever since I was old enough to hold a hammer, engineering contraptions of all sorts fascinated me. By nine or ten I had made several scooters with roller skates, attaching half a skate to the front of a 2x4 and the other half to the back. Then I'd nail a wooden apple box to the front, with two small boards attached on top for handles, and away I'd go. I had more fun building them than I did racing the neighbor boys.

Herb told me this engine was formerly used by the Navy to drive generators for radio batteries on battleships. He had found it in a second hand store. Next to the engine sat a couple of small wheels.

"Can I have those wheels too?" I asked.

"Yep," he answered, "and I'll help if you need me."

Herb suggested I find an old bicycle and cut the body to size. When he left to go flying, I jumped on my hack and headed for Everett in search of a frame. At a bicycle repair shop I spotted an undamaged specimen in a junk pile and bought it along with a second hand seat for 50 cents.

After cutting down the skeleton with a hack saw, I asked Herb to demonstrate how to weld. With a little practice, I created a reasonable facsimile of a motorcycle frame. A few days later, Herb presented me with a gas tank he had pounded out of a five gallon can (there wasn't anything he couldn't do). It took several months on my days off to complete the motorcycle which Herb clocked at 35 mph. Brother Cal was one happy kid.

I suppose my life could have forked down one of two paths at this point. Though the Twenties were past, some women still cropped their hair, donned men's pants, and threw themselves into adventures about which their mothers would have never dreamed. Most, though, eventually became traditional homemakers. I too might have succumbed, had not an opportunity presented itself.

Brother George and Gladys with some of her home built toys.

Gladys' brother Cal with his motorcycle that Gladys built.

Gladys' Latest Gadget!

* * * * * * * * *
Bellingham's Daredevil Girl Turns Machinist Much
to Delight of Little Brother and Sister

—Photo by Biery.

Gladys Dawson, Bellingham's 21-year-old daredevil girl, has turned machinist.

Her new avocation is much to the liking of her younger brother and sister, Clarence, 11 and Violet, 13, who reside at 1933 Humboldt Street, with their mother and sister. The immediate fruits of her machinist fad were showered upon Clarence and Violet recently in the form of a "half-pint" motorcycle, built by Gladys in the workshop of friends in Everett. The machine and its maker are pictured here.

"It took me five months to do it," Gladys admits. "I worked on it just one day a week, my day off," Gladys is an employee of the Leopold Hotel Coffee Shop.

"Of course, I didn't manufacture all of it," Gladys continues. The engine is of a type discarded by the United States Navy – it was originally used to drive generators which charged radio batteries aboard battleships. The frame is made of bicycle frames, hammered out and welded together. The gas and oil lines are pieces of tubing bought at second-hand stores and shaped as desired. The gas tank was once a tin can of some sort, Gladys doesn't know just what.

"The kids get a great kick out of it," she says. "It will travel at the rate of thirty-five miles an hour and, of course, they're not allowed to get out on the highways with it. Clarence can handle it awfully well, though, and I don't think he's ever have any trouble, even in traffic."

The pee-wee motorcycle stands just twenty-nine inches from street to seat. It is three feet, eleven inches long, and the wheels, airplane wheels, are eighteen inches in diameter.

Gladys is a motorcycle enthusiast herself. She belongs to two motorcycle clubs, the Mount Baker Motorcycle Club and the American Motorcycle Association.

"I can tell people my age, now without fear of losing my job," she gloats. "Two years ago I was entered in the Sehome hill motorcycle climbing competition and told a reporter that I was only 19. When the story was printed I lost a position in a restaurant where I had told the manager I was 21."

She's an aviatrix , too, and has her student's pilot license. She made her first solo flight at Tulip Field on the Ferndale highway, but she has to look at the engraving on the back of her wrist watch–given to her in honor of the event–to find out that it was made in 1931, when she was 16 years old.

That's not all, either! Following receipt of her license, she made a barnstorming tour through Eastern Washington and Oregon, making seventeen parachute jumps at aviation exhibitions. She still has two 'chutes at home which she keeps in perfect condition just in case some of the boy friends ask her to go for a spin in their plane.

A week ago Gladys took her first glider ride in Everett.

"They towed me around the field a couple of times with the glider rope attached to the rear of a car, so I could get the feel of the controls," she explains. "Then I cut loose and glided around over the field. I only got about four hundred feet of altitude during the flight, but it was lots of fun. Next I'm going to build myself a glider."

"Joe Smith says there's a two or three year old Travel Air 2000 for sale," Herb told me over a cup of coffee one day. "Only four hundred bucks. Wish I had the cash."

Built by Travel Air Manufacturing Company of Wichita, the prototype of the aircraft Herb described first flew in 1925. This particular Travel Air 2000, NC4850, boasted a Curtis OX-6 water-cooled, 100hp engine, the first of its type to be manufactured with dual ignition—a hot machine.

I felt a surge of excitement. Since my parachuting days, I had saved $300. Why couldn't I buy it? I put on my only suit and headed to the Bellingham First National Bank. The loan officer shook my hand and offered me a seat. "I own a 1934 Harley Davidson," I told him. "Could I use it as collateral for a $100 loan?"

The official cocked an eyebrow above his wire rimmed glasses. It wasn't often he met a twenty one year old girl owning a brand new Harley. "Yes," he replied after a moment's deliberation. "I think that would be satisfactory. What do you want the money for?"

"An airplane," I answered.

His expression changed, as he briskly, gathered the application forms. "I'm sorry, but Bellingham First does not loan money for the purchase of airplanes." That was that.

Desperate, I went to see Pop Place, the only person I knew who might loan me money. When I paid off the Harley a year ago, he noted with some surprise that I was more prompt with payments than most men. Even though I hadn't seen the plane, Pop smiled at my nervous request and said, "You go look it over. If you think it's worth the money, Gladys, you can count on my $100."

The next afternoon Herb and I methodically went through the plane. He liked what he saw; I loved it. We gave the owner a $25 down payment until I could arrange for the rest of my funds. By four p.m. the next day, we had completed the deal. Herb flew the Travel Air back to Everett (not wanting me to fly in the dark), and I rode my hack home on cloud nine.

That next Friday Herb and I headed for Forks, a tiny logging town on the Olympic Peninsula. Barnstorming this predominantly Indian community always brought in big cash; these folks just loved to fly. No sooner did we spin one customer around the sky and back, before another five dollar bill would flash under our noses. We hit Forks two weekends in a row, taking in enough after buying gas to pay off Pop. Now I owned my Travel Air free and clear. I was truly a pilot (albeit unlicensed) in a brand new industry.

Life in aviation was tough, though, even for a diehard like Herb. Prohibition lifted in 1933, and small breweries sprung up all over the Northwest. An offer for the distributorship for Hop Gold Beer in the Wenatchee area eventually proved too tempting for Herb. He and his childhood friend, Jimmy Windust, agreed it would be a great opportunity.

Since Herb's beer business was grueling work and six hours from Bellingham, I saw little of him. But his daily letters helped fill the gap. The postman made an event out of delivering them to the delight of the neighborhood children. If Herb didn't illustrate every envelope with color cartoons like Popeye and

Gladys and Herb with Travel Air 2000 at Forks, WA - 1934.

Jugs, he invented his own. One of my favorites was a fat, little sailor boy, holding my address in a boat.

Many of Herb's letters were romantic. Like most guys, Herb could express his feelings better in writing than in person. "I miss you Gladys," he'd write. "Wish you were here." I know Herb yearned for a like response, but I was wary, still afraid men weren't to be trusted.

To fill my days that summer, I continued to fly out of Everett when I could find a licensed partner to prop the plane and come along. After my friend, Lloyd Bengston, and I flew one day, we got to reminiscing about our barnstorming days on the Peninsula. When I confessed my burning desire to wing walk (it was catching on like wildfire across the U.S.), Lloyd didn't miss a beat.

"Let's go to Forks next weekend and give it a try!" Thank goodness Herb was in Wenatchee. If he didn't want me parachuting, he certainly wouldn't want me doing this.

As we approached Forks in my Travel Air the following Saturday morning, I pulled myself onto the wing and inched along her front spar by gripping guy wires that felt sharp as piano wire, even to my gloved hands. Buffeted by the wind, I knew if I lost my footing, I'd step though the fabric and fall to my death. When I finally reached the wingtip, I wrapped my left arm around the strut, leaving the other free to wave. I signaled "thumbs up" to Lloyd, and we dropped toward the toy town, buzzing it twice at treetop level. When Lloyd opened and closed the throttle to attract attention, I waved exuberantly, smiling my most beautiful smile. By the time we landed at the airfield, people lined up to talk to me, the perfect opening to sell rides.

With the summer over and holidays coming, Herb pled with me to spend Thanksgiving with him in Wenatchee. I wanted to go but couldn't shake the feeling it was a bad idea. The roads could get nasty over the Cascades, and the Harley had no windshield. Besides, was it wise to trust Herb?

I finally agreed, leaving early Wednesday morning, so I could be in Wenatchee by mid-afternoon. A fine winter rain fell until I neared the summit of Snoqualmie Pass where it turned to hard,

48

driving snow. The wet, two-lane highway turned into a nightmare of slush and frozen ruts. By the time I reached the summit, I was sliding out-of-control with both feet extended to keep upright. Freezing cold, I doubt I could have put on enough clothes to keep warm. My goggles were worthless as the snow stuck to the glass, effectively blinding me. I slid down the east side of the mountain into Wenatchee, guided only by the certainty that Herb would be waiting with a cup of hot chocolate, a T-bone steak dinner, and a hot bath.

Dark windows greeted me as I turned into Herb's driveway, and the front door wouldn't budge. "What now?" I wondered, mustering what strength I had left to kick start the Harley. I cruised by the Hop Gold office, finding it shut tight for the holiday.

Exhausted, I began a systematic search of main street, stopping at every tavern advertising Hop Gold. Each bartender told me Herb had bought rounds for the house earlier but had left some time ago. Finally I hit pay dirt. An old friend told me he'd seen the police pick up Herb for drunk driving. No doubt he was sleeping it off at the city jail.

The man I found being released by the desk sergeant was a far cry from the Herb of my dreams. Reeking of liquor, eyes bloodshot, he tried but could not justify his actions. We sat through long silences and strained conversations that weekend. The thought of waitressing at the Leopold looked pretty good in comparison. As I started home Sunday with a new chain for better traction, I swore I'd never again risk my safety for that big oaf.

By spring of 1936 Hop Gold Beer folded. Herb returned to Everett, paid me a visit, and charmed his way back into my good graces. Life moseyed along quite normally until August when Herb cooked up a great idea. He needed to pick up a Waco in Wenatchee, and his 6'3" friend, Shorty, wanted some cross country experience.

"Why don't you and Agnes take the train to Wenatchee," Herb suggested, "and meet us at the airport?" It sounded good to me since I'd never been on a train.

Agnes and I left early, drinking in the beauty of the Cascades from the luxury of a train seat. We started getting a little nervous, though, after we arrived in Wenatchee, walked to the Wenatchee Airport and waited three hours with no word from the guys. Finally, a clerk called out, "One of you gals named Gladys? You have a phone call."

"Shorty and me crashed in the mountains east of North Bend," Herb told me.

"Where are you?" I asked, sick with the realization he could have died.

"Get back to Everett," he responded. "I'll tell you everything at home."

With no money between us, Agnes and I decided to hitchhike. I didn't care how we got home; I needed to see Herb, to be sure he was safe. It didn't take long for a motorist to pick us up. He dumped us at North Bend, and we found another ride straight to Herb's house. When we walked in the door after 9:00 p.m., we found the guys in Herb's kitchen, drinking coffee and worrying about us. For once I think I hugged Herb tighter than he hugged me. The guys poured coffee, fixed sandwiches, and sat us down to tell their story.

As they left Everett in a 37 1/2 horsepower Taylor Cub, they told us, the pass had fogged in, so Shorty climbed to 6,000 feet to get on top of the cloud cover to look at the mountain tops cutting through the clouds. Suddenly, the engine lost power, and he couldn't maintain altitude. Once the plane dropped into the moist air, though, the engine perked right up, and Shorty once again pulled above the clouds. The third time this happened, the engine continued to lose power fast.

Herb took over the controls, trying to maintain normal glide speed in the fog by sound and feel. When it got dark, he sensed the ground rushing to meet them so pushed open the door for a look. A pine limb streaked by... Herb yanked back the stick to stall the plane.

With almost no jar, they stopped. Herb looked at Shorty, then opened the door again to see a forty foot drop off to his right. "You're not gonna believe this," he told Shorty.

The airplane, rocking precariously, had straddled a limb in a huge pine tree, the left gear on one side and the rest on the other. How on earth would they get down in one piece?

"Try to reach my toolbox," Herb told Shorty. "But be careful!. Don't rock the plane." For once Herb's habit of carrying tools with him paid off. Somehow, the two disconnected the control cables without destabilizing the craft and lowered themselves to the ground.

After a quick look around, they walked downhill for three miles before coming to a logging railroad. By a stroke of luck, a logger in a hand car was riding down the track. He slowed, unsure of what these two strangers wanted. They flagged him down, hitched a ride into the logging camp and another into North Bend.

Herb and Shorty swapped theories with us about what went wrong. They later concluded that carburetor ice formed as a result of condensation in the narrow passage into the carburetor venturi, cutting off air flow air, reducing power output, and choking the engine.

The more we discussed the accident, the more sober we four became. More men and women had disappeared on mountain flights than we cared to admit.

Taylor Cub 40 feet up in a fir tree. Cascade Mountains 1936

Chapter 5: Cross Country on Two Wheels

A fog hung over Bellingham, Washington, on the morning of September 1, 1936. The drizzling rain kept most folks indoors, but Madeline and I straddled my new Harley 45. A year had passed since Herb crashed in the Cascades. Since then Madeline and I had spent every waking minute either squirreling away money for our trip or planning it. Today was the big day. We had both saved $150 for expenses and would tour the American Continent for three months. Mayor Brown, members of the Chamber of Commerce and acquaintances gathered in front of City Hall to send us off.

Giving us a big hug and kiss, while onlookers chuckled, our bachelor mayor said, "Good luck!"

"Thanks," I answered, then kick-started my hack, put her in gear, and nosed into heavy downtown traffic.

Soon the noise of the city fell behind as we cruised along the highway. Against my side sat the reassuring weight of my Colt automatic next to letters of introduction given us by Mayor Brown. We weren't sure where we were going, but we headed over the Cascade Mountains where, we were told, the sun always shines.

My friends wondered what gave us the nerve to take off alone, two unescorted girls on a risky adventure. We weren't really that odd. Many women at this time felt rebellious, insisting they could do the same things as men. We had read about them, heard talk about them and even met one or two. This was especially true in the aviation industry with pioneers like Amelia Earhart, Katherine Stinson, Bobbi Trout, Pancho Barnes and my hero, Harriet Quimby.

America's first licensed woman pilot, Quimby was not the rough dare-devil you might expect. She was a stunning green-eyed brunette who worked in New York as a drama critic for

Leslie's Weekly . At twenty seven she grew bored with theater and started flying lessons in 1911.

To disguise her sex, the petite Harriet wore a large hooded parka until she crash landed one day just after take-off. Newspaper reporters arriving at the crash-site found the uninjured pilot to be none other than the petite drama critic. Now a celebrity, Quimby

MAYOR LIKES JOB
His Honor Kisses Two Local Girls As They Start Tour

"I'm liking this job better every day," Mayor W. P. Brown remarked Tuesday morning just after he had planted kisses on the rosy cheeks of Gladys Dawson and Madeline Thompson, two Bellingham girls starting on a motorcycle tour of the continent. The girls, with sleeping bags and other luggage strapped on the back of Miss Dawson's powerful motorcycle, sped away from the city hall at 11:35 a.m. on a trip that they plan will take them through every state in the Union and to Mexico City.

"It's an old Irish custom of wishing you Godspeed," the mayor remarked as he planted a fatherly smack (hissoner is a bachelor) somewhere between the edge of Miss Dawson's white helmet and her chin. He then stepped to the side of Miss Thompson and repeated the movement. Everyone blushed, even the reporters. The young women said they would only ride as far as Seattle Tuesday as special leather coats they are having made for the trip will not be ready before night. Wednesday they will head eastward, zig-zagging across the northern tier of states and making their way into the southland before the severe weather sets in.

Miss Dawson is an expert motorcycle rider. She has also soloed in an airplane and has made a number of exhibition parachute jumps.

went on to encourage other women to fly in articles she published in *Leslie's Weekly*. "In my opinion," she wrote, "there is no reason why the aeroplane should not open up a fruitful occupation for women...."

The Dresden-China Aviatrix, as newspapers described the journalist, made up her mind to cross the English Channel. Only two pilots, both men, had flown it solo. Against the advice of her British friend, Gustav Hamel (who even offered to dress in her clothes and make the flight), Quimby braved the dangers of the Channel weather and landed 25 miles south of Calais on April 16, 1912.

Harriet was killed shortly after the channel crossing at a Harvard Boston aviation meet while flying at only 1,500 feet. Her fragile Bleriot monoplane encountered rough air which tossed Quimby and a male passenger from the craft—unfortunately, early aviators did not wear seat belts. Her death confirmed critics' beliefs that women were not suited to flying.

By the time I came along, Quimby had become a legend in flying circles. Through stories told to me, I had picked up enough of her adventures to want to be like her. She gave aspiring women aviators the courage to believe we could do it.

Madeline and I may have been small potatoes in comparison, but we sure believed in being modern. The exhilaration of topping Snoqualmie Summit and dropping east into sunshine was almost as thrilling as jumping from an airplane. We stopped the first night at Soap Lake, a popular health resort near Wenatchee, Washington. Because this was rattlesnake country, we camped near the lake, hoping water would discourage the reptiles. That night gazing at the Milky Way, I believed I could do anything. Dad's huge influence seemed to recede to a pinpoint like the flickering star on which I focused my sleepy eyes.

The little dive bombers keeping us company that night left us lumpy with mosquito bites the next morning as we set off for Spokane. We made town just in time to catch Spokane Motorcycle Club members leaving for Glacier National Park. "Why don't

Gladys and Madeline start their 3-month motorcycle trip - September 1, 1936.

you tag along?" they asked.

Apprehensive, probably because of my childhood, I often avoided meeting people. But these were the first of many across the U.S. who welcomed us with open arms. Faced with such warmth, how could I not agree? We joined 40 other cyclers, crossing the Pend O'Reille River on a ferry and later eating hot dogs in open camp, drinking in the scenery of the Park.

The next two days we rode southeast through Montana to Yellowstone Park. A flat tire slowed us down in Butte; too bad all of our difficulties were not so easily fixed. I carefully patched the tube, bolted on the wheel and inflated the tire with a hand pump. The process took time, but we did it alone, making us enormously proud.

We paid a dollar entrance fee at the park's north gate and swung along scenic winding roads. Crisp air stung my cheeks as we climbed higher and higher to the Grand Canyon of the Yellowstone. The temperature only 18 degrees, we quickly abandoned our sleeping bags for a snug cabin. Early the next morning, we set off for Old Faithful.

"Gladys," Madeline whispered when we pulled in. "Look at that!"

I couldn't respond. Boiling water burst from the pool in a gushing column and then slowly receded in a cloud of steam. I'd never seen anything like it. Compared to the coast's monotonous rain and choking vegetation, the brute power of Old Faithful was

Glacier Park with the Spokane Motorcycle Club - 1936.

57

Old Faithful in Yellowstone Park - 1936.

astounding. The enormity of the Wyoming landscape unfolding before my eyes, mirrored an equally large landscape opening inside of me. The possibilities of life seemed limitless.

The next leg of our journey brought frightening weather. Our first day out of Salt Lake, we encountered a blinding dust storm similar to the Dust Bowl storms I'd read about in the newspaper. Our bodies and clothes saturated with dirt, we finally holed up in Rawlins, Wyoming, to wait out the storm.

Once the dust settled, we hit the road again, only to run into a swarm of grasshoppers pelting our faces and helmets like hailstones. Cars had pulverized the insects, greasing the highway and making travel deadly. Barely out of that mess, we spotted a electric storm headed our way. With lightening ripping the dark sky, I opened-up the Harley for Omaha.

Unwilling to admit I was a bit shaken, I welcomed a two day break but hesitated discussing the hazards we had faced with Madeline. "Should I have brought her?" I asked myself. "I'm used to bikes, but can she take it?" I felt a little embarrassed at breakfast when Madeline said, "Let's get going. I'm bored!" Back on the road with the Harley-Davidson factory in Milwaukee our next goal, we splashed out of Omaha over washed-out bridges and flooded roads.

One stop we didn't plan came in Spencer, Iowa. The town bustled with the excitement of a county fair, and we just couldn't resist. Madeline and I parked the bike and wandered to a field next to the fairgrounds where people flocked around an enormous balloon. Fascinated, I watched. The owners had dug a large pit in the ground and filled it with straw. At least 30 participants ringed the pit, each holding the bottom edge of the balloon. To the horror of the spectators (and to my delight!), a man struck a match, igniting the straw, which quickly filled the balloon with hot air.

With the envelope full and increasingly difficult to manage, a man wearing a parachute walked to the edge of the pit and grabbed a three-foot- long pipe, resembling a trapeze, secured

Inflation and lift off of homemade balloon at Fair in Spencer, Iowa - 1936.

by ropes to the balloon. When he yelled, "I'm ready," the balloon shot up like a bullet. At about 2,000 feet he let go, dropping a good 500 feet before his chute opened. Having hung above the earth myself, I knew he possessed tremendous courage. I heard people saying, "Crazy fool," but promised myself as we left Spencer that someday I too would fly a balloon.

We discovered finding sleeping quarters became a challenge at times between Spencer and Milwaukee. After a two day stay with Madeline's aunt on a farm in Raymond, Minnesota, we camped late the following night next to a beautiful, lake. It looked ideal, that is until I awoke the next morning between two graves, solemnly dressed in bouquets. From then on, we made camp in the daylight.

The next night when we pulled into Portage, Minnesota, the rain blasted us with the force of a fire hose. We cruised past a city park with a grandstand, and I pulled around to investigate. "Do we dare?" I asked Madeline as we wandered down the bone-dry benches. Dripping wet, she just nodded.

"Hey! What are you two doing?" said a harsh voice, startling me awake the next morning. I rubbed my eyes and focused on a policeman with a billy club standing over us. Someone had reported two vagrants sleeping in the grandstand. We talked fast for fifteen or twenty minutes before the amused officer walked off telling us, "Be careful girls. And...good luck."

We reached the Harley Davidson Factory in Milwaukee on September 24. The head of public relations gave us the royal treatment, including a guided tour of the factory and a tune-up on the bike, complete with a full gas and oil tank. I bet he figured we were the best advertisements Harley could get.

The next morning we visited Milwaukee's mayor, Mr. Hones, one of the few we found in his office. In no hurry, he questioned us about our trip and the Northwest. Thrilled when he asked us to sign his guest book, we added our John Henry's to a slate of dignitaries including General Pershing, Admiral Byrd and Charles Lindbergh.

Sleeping in bandstand, Portage, Minnesota.

Madeline and Gladys visiting relatives in New York City - 1936.

We cruised Chicago, second largest city in the U. S., the next day. For two small-town Westerners, the rush of traffic on Michigan Boulevard, the natives hurrying back and forth in the loop district, and the towering skyscrapers squeezed close together both excited us and brought on a giant case of claustrophobia.

Glad to leave the Windy City, we traced the shoreline of Lake Michigan for many miles before angling cross-state to the Canadian border and Niagara Falls. Climbing off the bike, we stood for what seemed hours, watching the water quicken its pace as it neared the precipice and shoot into space before dashing against the rocks below.

Until now we had enjoyed classic fall weather, but the mercury dropped below freezing on our way to Maine, pushing us south through Boston, Providence, New Haven and Bridgeport to New York City in hopes of finding sunshine and flowers. Before we left home, friends warned us about unfriendly New Yorkers. We were pleasantly surprised the morning we hit town. Pedestrians waved vigorously as we made our way through town. Laughing at the joke on the folks back home, we discovered five blocks later, when we met a wave of oncoming traffic, that we were driving up a one-way street.

Having crossed the American continent to see New York, we intended to get our money's worth. Staying with Madeline's

Pan Am Clipper at Floyd Bennitt Field, New York - 1936.

Gladys with sausage trees in background - 1936.

relatives, we shopped at department stores stocked with exotic merchandise, ate at the Automat (imagine food coming out of a coin operated machine!!), rode the subway snaking beneath the city, marveled at the beauty of Times Square at night, talked with Jack Dempsey, and visited Floyd Bennett Field and Coney Island. This whirlwind tour might exhaust some visitors, but we were young, strong and curious.

Like most tourists, our first stop had to be the Empire State Building. We pulled the bike right to the front entrance and walked into the packed elevator with our helmets still on. One man stared at me. When I turned and looked at him, he said, "Are you girls or boys?"

Without cracking a smile, I answered "That's sure an insulting thing to ask a fellow." Everyone just howled with laughter when my voice gave me away. With the ice broken, everyone began asking questions.

We left New York through the Holland tunnel, stopping off at Newark and Washington D.C. The South beckoned, though, so we flew through Virginia, West Virginia, Tennessee, and Kentucky. The rain came down so hard by Cardenas, N.C., that we rented a cabin to dry out our baggage, then walked downtown to see a show. On the way back a patrol car pulled behind us. "What you gals doin' heah," an officer asked through the rolled down window. When I told him, he said, "Git in. We're takin ya'll back. This ain't no place for gals to be walkin'." Apparently we had chosen a rough, black neighborhood to walk through. Seldom confronted with racial tension in our little Northwest towns, we had much to talk about in bed that night. Everyone, including blacks, had been so polite to us this day that we were somewhat puzzled by the officers' comments.

It had been raining for days by the time we reached Brunswick, Georgia. Tired of fighting the wet, we shipped everything but the basics to my relatives in San Diego. We awoke the next morning to another downpour. The Harley's spark plugs were so wet I had to dry them to get the bike started. "Remember our friends told us the sun always shines east of the Cascades?" Madeline laughed as we climbed on. "Yeah," I said. "Guess the sun doesn't shine all the time in Dixie after all."

St. Augustine, Florida, the oldest city in North and South America, held our interest long enough to tour Fort Marion, the House of Three Flags, and the Fountain of Youth. But we quickly continued to Miami, passing the Daytona Beach race course and arriving in time to reach the Miami dealership before closing time and make plans with some fellow Harley riders. They couldn't take us to the Keys as a hurricane had just washed out the bridges. But we spent the several days at sugar-sand beaches, taking in the blue ocean, the pink and orange coral and Florida's bizarre Sausage Trees.

The morning we left, our new friends rode with us on the Tamiani Trail through the Everglades, crawling with turtles, snakes, alligators, and other strange creatures to the eyes of two native Northwesterners. Stopping at a small Seminole village, we could see the natives had adapted well to their home. For safety, they lived in huts built on stilts ten feet above the water. To get in the door, they climbed directly from their boat onto a rope ladder which they pulled up after them.

The natives seemed friendly enough until I asked if we could take their pictures. Then men, women, children—everyone— vanished into their homes! "What did we do?" asked Madeline.

"They'll be back," one of our new friends answered. "They're

Visiting with the Seminole Indians in Florida - 1936.

dressin' up." Fifteen minutes later, the families proudly posed in full ceremonial regalia while we snapped pictures.

These people reminded me of the Indians back home, some of whom were family friends. They were decent, proud people who hadn't always gotten a fair break. Beginning to really grasp what it meant to be an American, I thought of all my fellow countrymen—the mid-Westerners, the Chicagoans and New Yorkers, the black and white Southerners, and now the Seminoles. I could see most folks are nice, warm hearted people who just want to get along.

Our route through the Deep South seemed a series of toll bridges and old fashioned ferries, pulled across streams with cables. I couldn't help but long for Herb as we burned up the miles. The guys we met in Miami were fun, but none had his devil-may-care sense of humor or Herb's manner that just told you he knew he could handle any situation. I had been gone almost two months, and I missed him terribly.

Near New Orleans the clouds parted, revealing the first sunshine we had seen in days. We took in some sights including the New Orleans levies, before heading through the sugar cane, cotton, and oil wells to Dallas, Texas, and its extravagant Centennial celebration. Madeline and I got to see one of our greatest heroines, world champion figure skater, Evelyn Chandler.

Leaving Dallas, we began the toughest but most thrilling part

One of many ferry rides we enjoyed - 1936.

of the trip, a six day trek to Mexico City. Our cross country adventure already seemed a big undertaking. But two women alone in Mexico felt downright dangerous. After visiting the San Antonio Mexican Consulate for passports and bonding the bike for three pesos (ninety cents), we crossed the border with a car caravan October 22.

On the first leg of our journey, a severe looking Mexican Customs Officer stopped us for questioning. Braced for the worst, I listened intently to his broken English. It sounded as if he wanted to know our destination, but I wasn't sure. I said, "I beg your pardon?" He instantly burst into a smile and replied, "Fine, fine." So much for communication.

The first night in Monterey, Madeline and I hit the town, catching a horse and buggy taxi to a wrestling match that sounded like fun. As the crowd gathered, we began to feel uncomfortable. The few women in attendance were definitely hussies, and men seemed to be casting steamy glances our way. We found later that polite women did not attend such sporting events. In spite of our discomfort we stayed put. Even though the match seemed gruesome, we had put out hard-earned money and didn't intend to miss a thing.

The next morning the caravan guide told us to expect a rough day. Service stations were about 150 miles apart, and we were to encounter steep gravel roads. With Valles our destination, we still had 200 miles to go at lunch time when we reached Victoria. Starving, we pulled up to a small cafe on main street and sat at a rickety table outside the front door. The only words we could understand on the menu were "soup" and "steak," but we soon learned that discretion is wise when ordering off Mexican menus. The chef, bearing no respect for the elderly, had selected a cow well past middle age. We did manage to bend the steak a bit with our knives and forks, but it was so tough we ate little. Still, we paid the owner, took up a couple of notches in our belts, and left for Valles.

The next day I aimed the Harley for Mexico City, climbing in low gear most of the way from 650 feet above sea level at

Valles to 8,000 feet on the plateau above. We clocked six hours and ten minutes, beating the cars in the caravan by 30 minutes. On the road we passed crews working in pairs with shovels and wheel-barrows. One worker carried a chunk of wood eight inches in diameter with two handles nailed to each side looking to be cut from a small tree. Using this primitive tool, he packed down the dirt and rocks dumped from the wheel barrow by his partner. Somehow my brand new Harley made this brute labor seem absolutely pathetic although I don't know if the Mexicans saw it that way.

Wet and very tired, we pulled into Mexico City after nine and a half hours. We stayed in a hotel for nine and a half pesos, took a good hot shower, and stuffed ourselves with the first edible meal since leaving the U.S. The hotel staff suggested we visit the pyramids, palace, cathedral, and floating gardens. They kept us busy that morning, but we were in Mexico City; we needed excitement. A championship bull fight scheduled that very afternoon seemed just the ticket. Arriving at the Toreador early, we found a large crowd waiting with officials searching the crowd for firearms before letting us enter the arena.

Bull fight in Mexico City, Mexico - 1936.

We had just located our seats in that mass of human bodies when a parade of six men came into the ring, each dressed in gaudy, tight-fitting costumes. Once they were positioned, a bugle sounded and a raging bull charged into the arena. I'm sure the bullfight is governed by an intricate set of rules, but to our uninformed eyes the animal was mercilessly tormented. Horsemen jabbed the bull with spears until it suffered great pain and was near exhaustion.

Then the fight commenced between the toreador and the bull. Waving a red cape to enrage the beast, the toreador would gracefully sidestep each mad rush. This continued to the shouts and encouragement of the crowd until the bull fell to its knees. At that moment, the toreador pulled out his dagger, stood fearlessly in front of the nearly dead bull, and stabbed it in the neck on its last feeble charge. Everyone cheered but us.

At dinner we tried the light and dark Mexican beer which tasted just awful. (Drinking for me came a few years later). We also tried to gag down some tequila, determined to be as grown-up as anyone, but it was worse. At least we could honestly tell our friends back home, "Yes. Of course we drank the local booze!"

The second morning, we began planning to leave. Told we could get motorcycle oil in Mexico City, we set out in search of a Harley shop. When Mr. DelCompo the dealer arrived, he couldn't speak or understand English, so a young man working for him interpreted. DelCompo seemed abnormally excited when we told him we wanted oil. Asking the young man what was wrong, he said, "Mr. DelCompo has never seen a woman in his shop before. He wants to know if you will wait while he goes home for his camera."

We had planned to just buy oil, but DelCompo insisted after taking snapshots that we let him check the bike over. "It's a long way to the United States," he said. "I don't want you to have any trouble." He refused pay for his work, saying it was a pleasure.

As we left Mexico City, a police officer, directing traffic at an intersection, waved us over. People had told us horror stories about Mexican jails ever since we left home. Pulling to the curb, I quickly told Madeline, "If he speaks English, act like you don't understand. I don't know what I've done, but that might help."

The officer combined his native tongue with sign language to communicate, but even my semester of Spanish in high school didn't help. As he spoke in a polite voice, he kept pulling his ear. By now a crowd had started to gather, growing to at least fifty before I decided his ear pulling indicated earrings. "He must be trying to find out if we're girls," I told Madeline.

"Si Señoritas," I told him, pulling off my helmet. Everyone had a good laugh, and then we roared toward home like a horse headed for the barn. The countryside back through Mexico was so densely covered with trees that it looked like a jungle. The open areas were alive with wild parrots of every imaginable color. But even in the midst of this, I found myself longing for the familiar Northwest landscape.

In Laredo the temperature had dropped to freezing, when six days before it had topped a hundred degrees. We picked up our luggage and roared across the Texas desert to El Paso where we replenished our oil supply, then pointed the bike toward Phoenix and San Diego.

Harley Shop in Mexico City. Madeline by bike - 1936.

After eight days visiting Grandmother Murphy and family in Southern California, we started down the home stretch November 10, hitting San Jose in time for the Armistice Day Parade. Making up for lost time after the parade, a police siren stopped us for speeding in Colait. The officer walked slowly to the bike, filling out a ticket as he proceeded.

"You boys know better than to drive 60 mph on this highway," he started. "May I see your driver's license please?" He looked at my identification, looked at us, looked at my identification, looked at us. Finally he said, "I had no idea you were girls!" He informed us about safety on the highways but, thank heavens, didn't ticket me. "Have a safe trip home," he said as he left.

The temperature dropped steadily as we drove without gloves through the redwoods to Garberville and on across mountains in ten degree temperatures to Roseberg. We bought gloves in Roseberg and stopped to gas up in Eugene with barely enough cash to take us into Seattle where Madeline's Aunt Claire lived.

After pumping gas, we visited the rest room. To keep warm that morning we had both pulled on every bit of clothing we owned, topping the mess with overalls. Obviously, a rest room visit was no small chore. I put my billfold on the window ledge while I wrestled with my clothes, thinking only of covering back up and getting warm in the service station. We visited with the station attendant in front of a wood burning stove for twenty or thirty minutes.

While chatting, I noticed a couple of women enter and leave the rest room, but by the time I remembered about the billfold, they were long gone—so was the money. All I could think of was, "What if this had happened in Mexico?" Between us we had $1.70 loose change in our pockets which got us to Aunt Claire's at 11:45 p.m. What a blessed feeling to be among familiar faces and to have good food, a hot bath and bed.

With a dollar we borrowed from Aunt Claire, we made Everett in time for lunch with Herb. His big kiss energized me more than a pot of coffee and three days' sleep. Revitalized, we continued to Bellingham and home.

Madeline and Gladys in San Diego, CA - 1936.

Two tired girls, Madeline and I had been on the road seventy three days (forty-four in the rain). We spent $305 for the trip but believed the money well spent. We learned more about ourselves in two and a half months than we could have in two years of college.

Chapter 6: The Proposal

After our cross-country escapade, home felt good, but I was flat broke. Back at the Leopold, I worked ten hours a day, six days a week, finding I needed my knee support to keep up the pace. (That parachute accident kept turning up like a bad penny.)

While hurrying to a table one day, I slipped in some water, dropping a T bone on the carpet and twisting my bad leg. When I tried to stand, red hot pain shot through my knee. Right then I knew I'd soon see the surgeon's knife.

That night the throbbing pain kept me awake. I thought back to my appendix surgery when I was seventeen and worked as a live-in housekeeper/cook for the Knights. One morning I awoke with a strange cramp in my side but managed to get Mr. Knight's breakfast and send the kids to school.

Mrs. Knight found me a little later on the couch, hugging my stomach. "Come on, Gladys, we've got to scrub the house today. The Johnsons are coming for dinner tomorrow night." When I didn't answer, she sat beside me and took my hand. "What's wrong, dear?" she asked.

The surgeons removed my appendix the next morning. I awoke a few hours later in a daze and uneasy with the white, antiseptic surroundings. Every thirty minutes or so, a business-like nurse would check my vital signs and ask the same question: "Do you want to urinate?"

"No!" I assured her. Having never heard the word before, it didn't sound like anything I wanted to do.

I don't remember how long this went on, maybe six hours. I only know I was ready to burst and too embarrassed to ask for help. With tears in my eyes, I finally told the nurse I had to use the bathroom. The bedpan she brought looked strange, but in my condition I would have welcomed a bucket.

Thank goodness I wasn't so naive this second time around. My physician told me the next day I would need to see a specialist in Seattle. The surgeon repaired my knee quickly a month later but required me to stay hospitalized for a couple of weeks. It could have been a lonely time; Mom didn't own a car, and I didn't know anyone in Seattle. But Herb strolled through the door every night around 7:00 with a Hersheys or a magazine and that big cockeyed smile. Before he left for home he would massage my feet.

Laying in that bed with my knee wrapped like a ham, I had a lot of time to think. Herb had wormed his way into my heart, even though I made up my mind a long time ago to never get close to a man. Dad made Mom's life miserable and kept the rest of us walking on eggshells. One horrible night Hilda sassed him in the living room, and he began hitting her. She screamed, cowering from his blows and insults. I couldn't watch a minute more

"Stop, Daddy," I cried, grabbing his arm. "Please stop!"

"So you want it too, you little brat?" he yelled, dropping his hold on Hilda and grabbing me by the hair. For two or three more minutes he worked me over with the razor strap. In tears Mom watched from a distance, knowing if she intervened, we'd get it ten time worse. I can't say I was afraid of him as much as hurt. Refusing to cow-tow like the other kids, I got most of his attention. Every day, it seemed, we would lock eyes as if he just dared me to try something.

Needless to say, I couldn't stay out of trouble. When I turned sixteen, Dad selected me as the one to pick up feed and supplies for the chickens in Ferndale. I discovered quickly if I revved the car engine and then turned the ignition switch off and on, it would make a neat bang, just like a firecracker. My mother heard me doing this and said, "Stop, Gladys. You're gonna get in trouble."

But I didn't listen. On the way home with a load one day, I just had to hear the bang. Immediately after, a disturbing rumble replaced the engine's quiet purr. I knew without looking I had either knocked a hole in the muffler or blasted it off—a death sentence for sure.

My only salvation was that Dad wasn't home. I told Mom right off, knowing if anyone could help, it would be her. After hearing my story, she walked to the cupboard and grabbed a coffee can where she hid her egg money. With shaking hands she pulled out some cash and sent me back to Ferndale. When the mechanic crawled out from under the car, I bent down for a look. The newly installed muffler sparkled so brightly, I knew I had a problem. Driving through a puddle on the way home, I thought, "That's what I need." I smeared abrasive mud all over the muffler, hoping it would camouflage the shine. Mom and I lived in terror for two months before we relaxed. Dad hadn't noticed a thing.

Dad deserted Mom in March of 1932, taking the money and leaving her with three kids, little food, and an unpaid mortgage. (By that time I had left home and was working for the Knights.) When I found out, I asked for Saturday and Sunday off. Strapping on my roller skates (not wanting to spend fifty cents for stage fare), I skated seventeen miles from Bellingham to Mountain View.

Mom and I cried in each other's arms, grateful Dad left but wondering what on earth to do. Mom had no money, no job skills, and almost no hope. Terrified that she would be evicted and homeless, we racked our brains until a neighbor told Mom of a clause in the Homestead Act that allowed financially distressed homeowners to stay a year in their homes before being required to leave. That combined with the little money I sent her, gave her desperately-needed time to make plans.

Now as I lay in my hospital bed, thinking back to those times, I realized Herb had broken through my defenses. When I first met him in 1932, he was nothing more than the means to an end. I must admit I found the man appealing, but Dad could be pleasant too in the company of strangers.

It must have been that spontaneous kiss after I soloed that disarmed me. When Herb threw his arms around me, my knees actually buckled. Unable to get that moment off my mind, I tried to attribute it to the magic of the moment. For five years I watched Herb carefully for a slip: a mean word, a push, something to reveal his true nature. Instead I found nothing but love and acceptance.

The day the hospital discharged me, I spent a few extra moments fussing with my hair. I wanted to look pretty, even though I hobbled on a pair of crutches. Herb drove me back to Bellingham on the most beautiful summer day I'd ever seen. The coastline seemed painted with water colors, the silver-tipped ocean on one side and little farms on the other silhouetted against the blue sky and green fields.

Herb must have sensed the time was right as we wound our way north. "Let's get married," he said.

Even though I thought he was kidding, I surprised myself. "Yes. Let's do," I answered. I turned and looked in Herb's eyes, realizing with a shock he was dead serious.

He pulled off the road and took both of my hands. "I think I've loved you since you crawled out of that cockpit the first time we flew," he said. "Your face was green, but you stuck up your chin and marched off to the hangar. I've watched you a lot when you didn't think I was looking."

He pulled me close and kissed me the way he had five years before. When we finally pulled back on the highway, the road ahead looked long and full of promise.

Chapter 7: Newlyweds

We drove home from the hospital, holding hands and making plans. Herb told me he had been hired at the Olympia Airport as a flight instructor and aircraft mechanic and would start in two weeks. We decided to marry, Depression-style, by skipping the formal wedding (who had the money?) and going to a Port Orchard justice of the peace.

Herb picked me up early August 4, our wedding day. While in the hospital I had asked Herb to find a buyer for the Travel Air because I knew I'd be on crutches for a long time. We sold the plane that day, took our vows a few hours later, and then headed north from Port Orchard to fish every river and stream on the Olympic Peninsula.

Actually I was flabbergasted when the justice of the peace pronounced us man and wife. Herb kissed my lips, took my hand and slipped on a thin wedding band. "What's this?" I whispered, tears flooding my eyes. Even though Herb had been forced to change jobs to save his two airplanes, he had somehow scraped together the cash for a ring. It couldn't have meant more if it had cost $100.

After a romantic night in Forks, complete with dinner and a beer, we left early for the Soleduck River. Herb pulled off the road in a spot he said "would not be too far to walk." He rigged both fishing poles, handed me my crutches, and set off through the brush.

In all his life, Herb never slowed down, and this day was no exception. Struggling alone through the underbrush, I felt sudden terror. "What made you think Herb would be different from Dad?" I asked myself. Climbing a big windfall, I slipped down the opposite side, wrenching my sore knee and bursting into tears. When Herb found me a few minutes later, he put two and two together.

"Sorry, Peach," he laughed, brushing off my clothes and hugging me. You know I love ya more than anything....even

Gladys and Herb's wedding picture - 1937.

fishing." I got the royal treatment that day—actually the rest of our marriage. We fished the Hoh, Clearwater, Queets and Quinault Rivers, eating trout for breakfast, lunch and dinner.

With two days left to find a place to live, we reluctantly headed for Olympia. After combing the town, though, we found nothing for rent. "Olympia's always booked-up tight," a waitress told us. "What do ya expect? It's the state capitol."

"What will we do, Herb?" I asked over a cup of coffee. My knee throbbed, and I felt a little panicky.

"Guess we'll have to leave town," he answered. "I can't think of anything else."

We headed south through Tumwater past the Olympia airport. About a mile out we finally found an auto court that rented one-room cabins by the week. Our first home offered a double bed, two-burner electric hot-plate, sink, drain board, and an outside john.

Herb came home three weeks later with good news. He had noticed a "For Sale" sign on a little two-room house across from the airport. "If you want it," he told me, "I'll add two bedrooms and a bath."

It didn't take me long to decide. The house looked pretty hopeless, but it sat on an acre of land. My imagination transformed it into a honeymoon cottage, com-

Herb fishing the Soleduck River on our honeymoon.

81

plete with an orchard, vegetable-flower garden, and white picket fence. Knowing Herb could quickly pound that house into shape, I said, "Let's do it!" We made the down payment with cash from my Travel Air.

A jack of all trades, Herb revamped the plumbing, electrical wiring, heating systems and cabinet work. You name it; he could do it. Although I desperately wanted to help, I found my crutches too cumbersome; I picked up nails and swept to keep busy. Even though Herb only remodeled before work and after dark, he had the two bedrooms and a bathroom usable in six weeks. My first hot bath was heaven.

Once Herb completed the addition, I busied myself with housework and cooking. I knew boiled or baked beans topped Herb's list of favorite foods. "When I was in the Navy," he had told me years before, "we'd pour syrup on the beans served with breakfast." When Herb asked me to make bean soup one morning before heading out the door, I decided to add sugar—actually, too much sugar. "How's that so different than syrup?" I asked later after the tears had dried.

Unlike cooking, gardening came much easier. The neighbors, who owned a greenhouse, shared lots of seeds, plants, and free advice. By the next summer, I had grown a magnificent garden. One fall evening after piling the corn stalks and cleaning the yard, I discovered my wedding ring gone. Herb found me sobbing at the kitchen table. "Don't cry," he said, wrapping me in his big arms and trying to put a smile back on my face. "Shoot, I've bought lots of them."

On our fifth wedding anniversary Herb replaced that missing ring with a two carat diamond. Though most women would die for a diamond, it never meant as much to me as the cheap band Herb put on my finger our wedding day. I put the new ring in a safety deposit box at the bank, wearing it only on special occasions to please Herb.

When not digging in the dirt, I set aside time to build a chicken house out of scrap lumber. Herb made certain to tell anyone who would listen that his beautiful wife had built that chicken coop. I suspect his boasting really came from a need to preserve his reputation as a carpenter.

While on crutches that first year in Olympia, I spent most of my time studying for my Private Pilot Certificate. Finally ready for the exam around Thanksgiving of 1937, I answered the ten essay questions in less than thirty minutes. The CAA Inspector graded them while I waited, asking me to verbally clarify any response he found to be unclear.

The flight test, (taken the same day) went just about as fast. The inspector told me to fly west of the airport and execute a two turn spin in each direction while he watched from the ground. On my return he boarded the plane and asked for a figure eight and two spot landings. That was it. I passed both tests. After five years of work, I could call myself a full-fledged pilot.

I continued studying as time permitted, passing the written examinations for my Commercial Certificate and Flight Instructor Rating before I logged the 200 hours required for my Commercial Flight Test. While the subjects were still fresh in my mind, I thought I might as well take the written exams for Ground Instructors Certificate which tested knowledge of aerodynamics, navigation, meteorology, civil air regulations, aircraft, engines, instruments and parachutes.

I knew all this knowledge would come in handy, but I had no idea how many doors it would soon open.

Chapter 8: Pulling Out of the Depression

Herb lived two lives: one at home and one at work. While I recuperated from my operation and studied for exams, Herb repaired aircraft, instructed novice pilots, sold gas, and did whatever needed done at the Olympia Airport. In short time, Cram Flying Service employees became one big family. Herb and I formed lifelong friendships with pilots who later became famous in aviation. To us they were just the gang.

Take Herb's boss, Jack Cram, for instance. A straight-backed, no-nonsense leader, Jack gave orders and expected others to carry them out. Having graduated from the University of Washington and later from Pensacola Naval Air Station as 2nd Lieutenant Naval Aviator USMC Reserve, Jack dressed immaculately, never leaving home without mirror- polished shoes and vertically creased shirts. Little did we know Jack would soon become a World War II hero.

Four years later in operations at Guadalcanal, Jack would win the Navy Cross and permanent nickname, "Mad Jack." At that time, October 15, 1942, troops at Guadalcanal were in a tight fix. Japanese battleships and destroyers had nearly decimated Henderson Field and crippled the majority of Marine aircraft remaining on the island. Twelve miles up the beach, enemy transport ships needed only to unload their troops to retake Guadalcanal. A May 1982 *Naval Aviation News* article, "Mad Jack Cram and the Blue Goose," describes the incident:

At 9700 on the 15th, thirty Zeros circled at 15,000 feet over the invasion area. The marines could scrape together only 12 Dauntless divebombers and 8 Wildcats to meet the threat. Major Jack Randolph Cram, personal pilot to Marine General Roy Geigers's PBY-5A, volunteered the "Blue Goose" for the attack. Normally the PBY was used only for transport, patrol, or reconnaissance, but Cram was not concerned that a PBY had never made a daylight torpedo attack. He mounted two 2,000 pound torpedoes on the wings and rigged wires from the cockpit to release them.

With no copilot and only five minutes of instructions on torpedo bombing, Cram launched the "Blue Goose" for the attack. One mile from the enemy fleet, he put the aircraft into a dive. Although the PBY-5A was built for a maximum speed of 160 mph, Cram saw 270 mph before he leveled off at 75 feet. While taking fire from Japanese transports and destroyers, Cram released his torpedoes-both were hits.

After he pulled off from the sinking transport, five Zeros attacked the Blue Goose. Members of the crew-Metz, Hoffman, Anderson, Kirby and Horton fought back with 30 caliber machine guns. Cram still had one Zero on his tail when he arrived at Henderson Field, but luckily, a marine in an F4F was geardown in the pattern and saw Cram's plight. The Wildcat extended his turn to final approach and shot down the Zero just as Cram landed.

Although the Zeros plugged the Blue Goose" more than 160 times, her unorthodox attack under the hands of Cram sank three transports and damaged several others. After Guadalcanal, Major Cram went on to command VMB-612, an experimental night bomber squadron.

A Marine officer at Guadalcanal commented, "If ever I saw a man with sheer guts, it was Jack Cram. He knew it would probably be his last flight, but he jumped at the chance." That was just Jack's nature. He took chances and always came out ahead.

Maybe that's why Herb and I took to Jack right away. He certainly knew how to surround himself with talent. Herb's first day on the job, Jack introduced him to Gwin Hicks, Jack's right hand man, whom he had met when they worked at the Washington State Highway Department. Gwin was to become the industry's best public relations man and Herb's business partner. A born salesman with a genuine enthusiasm for aviation, Gwin understood the power structure of business and government and knew how to use it. Gwin, Viv, and three-year-old, Jackie, would become our inseparable friends.

Bud Halloway, another good pal, came to the Olympia Airport by chance. He and a high school friend showed up at the hangar one evening, hungry and destitute. Traveling the country by box car, the boys decided to stretch their legs when the train stopped south of Olympia. Half a mile away when the engines start up, they sprinted back only to watch the caboose shrink to a pinpoint, then disappear down the line. They lost everything: money, clothing, sleeping bags, camera. After hearing their story, Jack fed the boys and put them up for the night. He liked Bud so much that the next day he offered him room and board if he would work as line boy while Herb taught mechanics at Olympia High School.

It didn't take us long to become fast friends with the gang. We'd congregate nearly every day after work. Sometimes Herb would bust through the door, shouting, "Gladys, throw some more plates on the table." Other times we'd eat at Bud's and Jack's since they were batchin'. (Guess who cooked?) If Viv and I couldn't face cooking, we'd all cross the street to Slegel's Tavern for a beer and dinner. I looked forward to weekends the most. Saturday nights meant dancing in Olympia with Gwin and Viv; we rarely left until the music stopped.

In spite of our night life, days kept Herb busy what with teaching and working at the airport. He had just stepped through the door one evening, dirty and exhausted, when Jack dropped by the house. Excited, he told us about a hangar the Works

Port Angeles airport - 1938.

Progress Administration (WPA) had just completed in Port Angeles, west of town along the Straits of Juan De Fuca. "There's not an airplane on the whole darned dirt field," he told us, "but everyone I talked to wants to fly!"

It wasn't long before Jack had made a deal with Clallam County to lease the facility which included an agreement to let us build living quarters in one corner of the hangar. Before we knew it, Herb and I were dividing time between Olympia and Port Angeles, scheduling students for the days we would be there.

As we drove along Hood Canal one day, returning from Port Angeles, Herb and I decided to eat our lunch at Dosewallips Creek. While I got out the picnic basket, Herb scrambled over rocks to the creek's mouth and began yelling, "Gladys, get over here!" The spot was thick with oysters. We filled our lunch sack and treated Viv, Gwin and Jack to a gourmet dinner that night. Needless to say, every trip after that we stopped for a fresh supply. While I gathered oysters, Herb liked to sit on a log, slicing the meat from the shell with his pocket knife and swallowing it whole. After watching him eat several, I said, "Herb don't you know they're still alive?"

"Yup," he said. "I can feel em wigglin' all the way down."

Although our days at Port Angeles usually relaxed us, we did face a few tense moments. One afternoon a young baseball player arranged for Herb to fly him across the Straits for an evening game in Victoria, Canada. When Herb called Canadian customs to ask for clearance, the controller told him, "Land at Lansdown Field." Herb did as instructed, only to have an overzealous customs officer confiscate the plane. "Why are ya doin' this?" Herb asked the sober young man.

"I'm charging you with making an illegal landing," he answered. "You should know that Lansdown's off limits to foreign traffic!"

This was one fellow Herb's friendly persuasion could not budge. In a rage, Herb found a pay phone and called a Canadian friend who advised him to calm down and contact Ottawa immediately. Even that didn't get immediate results. After numerous phone calls over the next three weeks, we finally returned by ferry to Victoria to pick up our prisoner-of-war.

The weather looked ominous when Herb and I prepared to depart from Victoria in the open-cockpit QCF Waco. "Shouldn't we wait a bit?" I asked.

"We'll be fine," Herb answered with that stubborn-as-a-mule look of his. I wasn't so sure. Dependent on the accuracy of our magnetic compass, we took off across twenty five miles of open water with clouds so low we could barely see half a mile in any direction.

Gladys and Herb with QCF Waco in Victoria, B.C. - 1938.

A steep bank stretches along the coastline from Port Angeles, broken near the city by a mile-long spit paved with a Coast Guard airstrip. I knew Herb was thinking the same thing as I: "Will we see the bank in time to turn and head for the spit?" I held my breath, staring intently into thick clouds. Suddenly the enormous wall loomed up, but Herb, his instincts perfect, swiftly turned to the east. Breathing more normally, I spotted the Coast Guard installation directly below.

As we landed, a commander hurried out to see who in the heck was crazy enough to be out flying in such weather. When he recognized Herb, he laughed and said, "What in the world you doin out there?"

"Not much," Herb replied. "Just testin' my eyes." They exchanged some good-natured bantering over a cup of coffee (to settle my nerves you understand). The male pilot, I was learning, never admits fear—he just embellishes his hangar stories with a few more hair-raising details!

It wasn't much later that I added a couple of stories to my own collection of aviation lore. One day, eager to get in some flying time, I snagged an available plane and headed to Bellingham with my friend, Marge O'Donnell. We flew along, enjoying the scenery, until I spotted an enormous airplane in a

Marg O'Donnell and Gladys checking out a bomber in a farmer's field.

farmer's field surrounded with military personnel. Wondering what was up, we landed our J3 cub close to the fourteen ton, Martin 10 bomber. The cub looked about as big as a fly speck next to the giant.

Crawling out of our cockpit, we walked up to two guards. The bomber's faulty engine had been repaired, they told us, but the plane couldn't lift-off because of soft, wet soil. We circled the bomber, watching the flurry of activity. So far a flight crew had unrolled landing strips resembling venetian blinds in front of each wheel. The commanding officer figured the 155 foot long lanes of slatted boards would give enough run to lighten the bomber for take off. We left, shaking our heads. A few days later, wind conditions must have been good. We heard the bomber took off and landed safely at McChord Field. Glad I wasn't the pilot.

Another day when I was practicing power-off stalls, my engine died. "Uh oh—I'm going down," I blurted out (as if there were someone to hear). If I said I wasn't frightened, I'd be lying. I put the plane in a glide like I'd been taught, checked out an open field below, and pointed her down. "At least there's no power lines," I thought as I cleared a barb-wire fence and bumped to a stop in the weeds. The airplane came out okay, but my ego took a beating.

"What killed the engine?" "Did I do something wrong?" I kept asking myself as I hiked to a farm house to phone the airport.

Martin B-10 bomber preparing for take-off after a forced landing.

If the mechanic set the idle too low, the engine could have died from the demand during the stall. But I suspected it died because I'd picked up carburetor ice.

It turned out I was right. Herb found me fast, once I called the airport. Hopping out of the truck a half hour later, he looked over the engine which checked out fine. "Looks like you made a perfect landing," he commented. "Want me to fly the plane back?"

"No way," I said.

"Let me prop you then. And don't forget you have carburetor heat," he added with a grin.

He didn't need to say that! I felt dumb enough. Carburetor heat had been recently added to engines, and I had forgotten to switch it on. You can bet I never did that again.

My studies continued through winter and early spring when I passed my Commercial Flight Test in March and Flight Instructor Exam in April, 1938, with CAA (Civil Aeronautics Authority) inspector, Jack Feeney. To our knowledge I was the only licensed woman instructor in the Pacific Northwest.

I basked in admiration from the airport crowd when I landed that spring day. After Herb snapped several pictures, I walked into the office smiling from ear to ear. Gwin, who was waiting, shook my hand and said, "Gladys, this is Margaret Thompson. She'll be your first student."

"Which cub shall I use?" I asked once we finished introductions.

"Oh! She has her own airplane," Gwin answered. "Her husband flew her over in their Taylorcraft."

My smile faded. I had never flown a Taylorcraft which wasn't so bad, except it had side-by-side seating and wheel control. All my flying had been in tandem aircraft with stick control. I tried hard to seem calm as we walked to the airplane. It's a good thing a student's first lesson starts with a pre-flight inspection. As I took Margaret through the procedure, I acquainted myself as best I could with the controls and instrument panel.

Before takeoff we set the altimeter to field elevation, set the trim, checked the carburetor heat and magnetos. I assisted Margaret with a somewhat sloppy takeoff (thank goodness she didn't know any better). After an hour-long flight, making turns, practicing altitude control and executing dutch rolls, we returned to the airport. Margaret stayed on the controls while I instructed her on the approach and landing. She did a good job for her first flight, but, I can tell you, I learned much more than she.

Having passed my initiation rite, I became a regular instructor with Cram Flying Service. The students came in all sizes and shapes and occasionally surprised us as well. One student, Dr. Dumachel, would drive weekly from Raymond, WA, for a flight lesson and evening ground school. One evening after class, the doc noticed Bud breathing heavily through his mouth instead of his nose. "Open your mouth wide, son," he said, "and let me have a look at your throat. You too, Gwin." He quickly examined each young man, then matter-of-factly announced, "I'll be coming up for a lesson next week. You boys be ready for a tonsillectomy."

We figured the doctor knew what he was talking about, so that next week, Bud, Gwin and Jack's brother, Ed (the doctor's newest recruit), lined up in the classroom, awaiting their turns. When Dumachel arrived with his black bag, one after another the boys climbed on the kitchen stool, opened their mouths wide, took their local anaesthetic, and tried to be brave.

Tonsillectomies are far messier than cooking stew we soon learned; I'm sure the boys would have preferred the latter. But the good doctor finished his job in no time, and the guys—a bit pale but still walking-trooped off to fill their prescriptions. "You boys go over to Slegel's and eat all the ice cream you want," Dumachel shouted after them. Then he cleaned up his instruments, put away the chairs, and converted his operating room back to a ground school classroom.

This spontaneity seemed natural at the Olympia Airport. Since its accommodations were attractive and its location directly in the north/south traffic lane, pilots flew in from everywhere. One of the most notorious was Herb's good friend, Tex Rankin. A cross country racer, Tex first made national news in 1929, setting a light plane, speed-distance record when he flew 1350 miles from Vancouver, B. C., to Mexico, in thirteen hours and seven minutes.

Tex and Herb's friendship hailed back to the post World War I era when Tex opened his first flight school in Walla Walla, WA. He later moved his flight operation to Portland, Oregon, in the late twenties after which he moved on to run the largest flight

Tex Rankin and Herb with Tex's aerobatic Great Lakes Bi-plane - 1938.

school in the nation at Tulare, California. He had become a legend in aviation circles.

Whenever he came north, Tex would stop to swap hangar stories with Herb. One particular day on his way to a Vancouver air show, Tex landed in his Great Lakes, followed closely by a friend flying an Ercoupe, a highly unconventional airplane. Equipped with castered wheels that would grip the runway (even when the plane crabbed into the wind), the Ercoupe also boasted a steering wheel in lieu of rudder pedals—supposedly making flying easy as driving a car down the road.

Engineers considered the plane unsuitable for aerobatics. So when Tex, in his soft, squeaky voice, bragged he could do anything in the Ercoupe he could do in his Great Lakes, I must have rolled my eyes or something. He didn't impress me—the guy looked more like a farmer than some hot-shot pilot.

"You don't believe me?" he asked.

"Come on, Tex," I answered. "That Ercoupe's not built for aerobatics."

"All right. Let's go up. I'll show you what she can do."

I couldn't resist the invitation, pretty sure Tex had gone too far. Was I in for a surprise. Tex looped, snap-rolled, executed vertical reverses and cuban eights—absolutely everything but spins—in that Ercoupe. After leaving my fingerprints permanently embedded in seat, I became a believer. I learned first-hand that the stories about Tex were true.

Chapter 9: Teaching at St. Martins

As the weeks and months passed at Olympia Airport, we got in the habit of tuning the shop radio to news broadcasts of the escalating war in Europe. The air fairly crackled with tension as Americans from coast-to-coast followed Hitler's march across the continent. Herb and I couldn't help wondering how we'd be affected by this distant conflict.

The war industry for U.S. allies had already bolstered the Northwest economy. Kaiser shipyards in Portland-Vancouver was increasing production, and Boeing Aircraft Company in Seattle was pumping out B17's (Flying Fortresses), adding thousands to its employee roster.

With all indicators pointing to war, everyone in the aviation business agreed the U. S. needed to move quickly to catch up with the rest of the world. In the twenty years from 1918 to 1938, our military had fewer than 5,000 pilots and maintained only 1,000 aircraft. The Army Air Corp had only one training base, Randolph Field, with the capacity to turn out 500 pilots per year; the Navy had Pensacola, with a similar capacity.

Civilian aviation also lacked competent training. Some 21,000 pilots were registered, but many licenses had lapsed. Fewer than 10,000 civil aircraft existed with only 400 in scheduled operation. By comparison, Germany boasted 65,000 pilots and technicians in training, Italy had 100,000 and France had 20,000.

I can't say Herb and I planned to take advantage of this situation, but when Jack accepted a position with the Civil Aeronautics Authority in Washington, D.C., the fall of 1939, we jumped at the chance. Jack offered Gwin the business if Gwin could pay off the mortgage. This included the hangar as well as ground leases from the City of Olympia and Standard Oil Company.

Once Gwin made the deal with Jack, he needed shop equipment and airplanes, so he invited Herb for a bull session over coffee. "Are you interested in a partnership?" Gwin asked.

First St. Martins CPTP secondary class at Buroker-Hicks Flying Service in Olympia. Instructor Herb on left. Chief pilot Howard (Brick) Wellman on far right.

"Sounds good to me," Herb said.

They agreed Herb would contribute his tools and two airplanes, and they'd buy Jack's cub trainer together.

Buroker/Hicks Flying Service made money from day one. We quickly snapped up the dealership for Piper Aircraft. That plus mechanical work in the shop floated us through the winter months. By spring we had so much business we had to buy more airplanes and hire extra pilots and mechanics.

Summer aviation news briefs reported that the Civil Aeronautics Authority would soon begin a national program of college-administered flight schools—just as we had suspected. Gwin immediately phoned Father Gerald Desmond of St. Martins College in Lacey, WA., to propose the college become involved and use Buroker-Hicks as its flight school contractor.

Father Desmond called us back shortly. "We're interested. I'll submit an application for St. Martins as soon as possible and keep you posted." We didn't wait long. As soon as test programs were run at eastern colleges and Purdue University, the C.A.A. certified St. Martins to offer a Civilian Pilot Training Program (CPTP). The college hired us to provide the aircraft, pilot instructors and maintenance.

With the CPTP contract in their pocket, Herb and Gwin bought three new Piper J3 trainers. They decided the least expensive way to get them from the factory in Lockhaven, PA, would be by air—but who would do the flying? Most pilots at this time would fly anything, anywhere, anytime if someone else would just put the gas in. This was the case when Gwin contacted three locals. "Would you fellows be interested in taking the train to Lockhaven and flying back three new Cubs?"

"You bet!" they replied in unison.

"Then plan on making the 2:30 train from Seattle tomorrow." One week later we had three new airplanes.

When news got out about St. Martin's new flight program, 20 students immediately enrolled, and Father Gerald needed a ground school instructor—right away. I'm sure the college expected a man since St. Martins was an all-male Catholic institution. Besides, women were supposed to be housewives! Imagine his surprise when he found through the grapevine I was the only available certified ground school instructor in the Northwest. Those exams I took on a whim a year ago paid off in spades!

As I nervously left my car the first day of classes, I wondered what was in store for me. Pushing my way through a sea of men, I sensed them gawking, so I walked with my eyes straight ahead. "What's *she* doing here?" I could hear them whisper. I was, after all, the first woman to teach at St. Martins. Even though I felt tense as a polecat, my first day in class went well, and within days my students had me scrambling to keep up with their

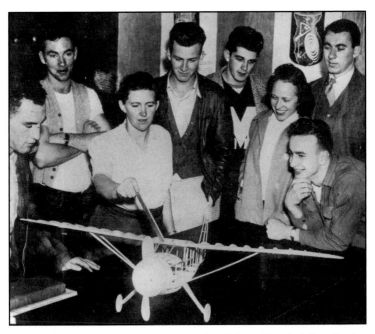

Gladys with her first students from St. Martins College. From left, Don Cooley, Frank Sinclair, Gladys, Neil Shannon, Ted Sumerville, (next two visitors) and Chuck Cleaver.

excitement and curiosity. More than anything, they wanted to fly. If a woman taught the class, so be it. I became known among the students as "Assistant Father".

One day Father Gerald walked into the classroom, his long black robe flowing behind his six foot frame. He smiled broadly, as he always did, but I stiffened at the podium for a moment, barely able to breathe. Before long I forgot he was there as I explained aerodynamics to my curious audience. As the students filed out, the Father stood up.

Ted Sumerville and Gladys, her first St. Martin's student to solo - 1942.

St. Martins school bus arrives with 22 students pictured with Buroker-Hicks Flying Service crew. Front row - Andy Anderson, Rudy Libra, Ken Lane, Tom Emerson, Jim Smith, Ken Ogden, Doc Curtis; 2nd row - Ted Sumerville, Jack Kearney, Gene Carter, Warren Keating, Roy McGraw, Charles Cleaver, Charles Bayah, Ron Sully, Bon Mullins; Standing - Ernest Barkley, Pat O'Grady, Herb Buroker, Father Gerald Desmond, Howard Wellman, Gladys Buroker, Bob Collins, Howard Peterson, Don Cooley, Neil Shannon, Bill Hutchison, Ray Brennan, Leo Bollis, Bob Escallier, Frank Sinclair, Stanley Trohimovich, Matt Kuran and Harold Chanbers. St. Martins students are underlined.

"I enjoyed your class tremendously," he said, adjusting the crucifix, dangling from a heavy chain around his neck "It would be such a pleasure to fly." I broke into a big grin, feeling like I'd just jumped over the moon.

The students' flying records and grades for our first class earned excellent evaluations from the CPTP National Office and also brought two additional classes to St. Martins: Pilot Instructor Refresher Course and Secondary Course. These courses marked a major departure in aviation training. Prior to this time, any transport pilot could teach student pilots. With these two courses, transport pilots' instruction became standardized with a flight instructor rating.

As the days ticked by, I became accustomed to my schedule. One morning, though, when the 5:00 a.m. alarm blared, I awakened overwhelmed with nausea. Herb found me ten minutes later with my head still hanging over the toilet. In spite of this rocky beginning, it was a happy day in February 1940 when the doctor confirmed my pregnancy. Except for a little morning sickness, I don't think I've ever felt better.

I continued teaching flight and ground school in spite of my bulky, lumbering body. Sally Rae was born October 4, 1940, three weeks after I said a temporary good-bye to "the boys." With my younger sister, Vie, helping out, life seemed like a bed of roses. While she did most of the housework, Herb refused to let me out of bed for the baby's night feeding, arguing, "You did your share the last nine months; I'll take care of her at night." And he did, changing her diaper and handing me a sweet-smelling bundle to feed.

As any mother knows, the first year with her baby can pass in a flash. But much had happened, and I knew my country needed me. My head still swimming with thoughts of dirty diapers and sterile bottles, I resumed teaching at St. Martins the fall 1941 and also taught a class of CPTP primary flight students.

As it turned out, this particular class would gain more experience than most. These students would start training at

Olympia near sea level, solo in Pasco on a snow-covered field, and complete training at Weeks Field in Coeur d'Alene, Idaho, with a field elevation of 2,250 feet.

Chapter 10: Preparing for War

September 1942

**AIR TRANSPORT COMMAND IS ESTAB-
LISHING GROUP OF WOMEN PILOTS FOR
DOMESTIC FERRYING STOP NECESSARY
QUALIFICATIONS ARE COMMERCIAL
LICENSE FIVE HUNDRED HOURS TWO
HUNDRED HORSEPOWER RATING STOP
ADVISE IF YOU ARE IMMEDIATELY
AVAILABLE.**

> **Henry H. Arnold**
> **Commanding General**
> **United States Army Air Forces**

Sundays Herb always slept late. Today, December 7, 1941, was no different. While I nursed two-month-old Sally Rae at the kitchen table, Vie put on the second pot of coffee, tucked a coffee cake in the oven, and chattered about her latest sweetheart..

"Rise and shine," Herb hollered from the bathroom.

"Rise and shine, yourself!" I answered, tickled that Herb still considered himself the early bird.

He staggered into the kitchen, hair standing on end, and flipped on the radio. Vie started to hand him a cup of coffee.

Throwing his arms around Vie's waist, he splashed coffee everywhere as he danced her across the room. A newsflash interrupted the program. "At 7:55 a.m. this morning" the announcer said, "Japanese torpedo planes and submarines attacked Pearl Harbor, devastating the Pacific Fleet and brutally killing hundreds of American sailors, marines, soldiers and civilians."

We listened in shock to the unfolding events. We knew the Pacific Northwest with Boeing, Kaiser shipyards, and all the naval and air bases could easily be targeted by the Japanese for attack. The next day in a radio address to the nation, President Roosevelt confirmed our worst fears. With one dissenting vote, Congress had declared war on Japan. We knew our lives would change dramatically in the next few years.

The region quickly geared up for attack. Crews installed sirens in every community, so citizens could practice air raid drills. Boeing Aircraft Co., an especially vulnerable target, camouflaged its entire complex by commissioning artists to paint a residential scene on the roof.

Everyone wanted to help the war effort. So did I. But when General Henry H. Arnold of the Air Force Ferry Command letter came soliciting women for the Ferry Command, I refused. I couldn't leave Herb and Sally. "I'll serve my country in some other way," I told myself. As it turns out, I did.

Shortly after Pearl Harbor, the Air Force notified Buroker-Hicks that the Olympia Airport, including hangar and weather station, would be occupied by a squadron of P-38's from McChord Field which descended on us like locusts a few weeks later. Security being vital, guards roamed the airport, even locking in the weather personnel during their shifts. Vie, who worked in the weather station, couldn't stand the soldiers ogling her when she went out to fly the weather balloons. She packed up and moved to Bremerton to work for the U.S. Navy.

To protect the airplanes in case of bombing, construction crews built revetments, circular mounds of dirt higher than the airplanes with openings just large enough to taxi into. The entrances were at a different angles, so only those aircraft facing the explosion would be damaged if the Japanese bombed the airport. By the time they finished their work, the field looked like an ant colony from the air.

The pilots were just kids, but could they fly. When the siren sounded for air drills, a few sprinted to the closer planes while others hopped onto transport jeeps which dropped them off at intervals. In minutes the entire squadron shot off like bullets and fell into formation. The siren sounded again and again, often when the guys were at mess.

Meanwhile our work at St. Martins took on new urgency as we became painfully aware that our students would likely be bombing the enemy or transporting supplies. With more students each term, we desperately needed more planes. To our relief, the national office of the CPTP telephoned one day with news that it had assigned the college some planes located in southern California. We were to pick them up.

By this time air command had ordered a sundown-to-sunup blackout west of the Cascades. That meant everything. Civilians could drive at night in an emergency but could not use headlights. Herb and I headed south with several pilots in a station wagon, stopping only for gas and food.

Late the first night I took the wheel, but couldn't see a thing, the night enveloping the car like black tar. In desperation I flipped the headlights on and off and immediately heard a siren. The patrolman's signalled for me to roll down the window. "Whatcha doing," he said angrily, "signalling the Japs?"

"No sir," I said, mentally kicking myself. "We're headed to California to pick up planes for the Civilian Pilot Training Program at St. Martins." Grudgingly he agreed to let us continue. "But keep your lights off!" he ordered before walking back to his car.

No sooner did we get our aircraft back to Olympia than Gwin told us we must move our operations to Pasco, Washington. With the coastal airways overloaded by the military, the CAA had decided to relocate nonmilitary operations inland to Eastern Washington and Oregon. While Gwin worked with the Pasco Airport Authority to secure a hangar, study hall and housing accommodations, Father Gerald arranged to bus the students, records, and teaching materials.

Even though the move required backbreaking effort, we settled in and got back to work. Our second year pilots, in spite of the move, graduated with top honors. The newspapers picked up the story, and in no time St. Martins College basked in public recognition. Not only was ours the smallest college in the CPTP but most highly rated—and the first to establish an extension campus for flying. We had just started to feel comfortable when Commander Creighton, 113th Naval District of Seattle, noted his Navy Cadets' exceptional performance at Buroker-Hicks Flying Service and decided the Navy would take over the airfield. Someone should have filmed Father Gerald's reaction—we had been in Pasco four weeks!

"This time I'm gonna find an air field where no one in his right mind would live," Herb said through clenched teeth as he drove off. He phoned us six days later. "I think I've found a spot in Coeur d'Alene. It's called Weeks Field." When Gwin, who had answered the phone, relayed that location to me, my heart sank. Idaho seemed so far off the beaten track. But he was right; who would want to live there. "The runway's 2,600 feet, and there's also a small hangar that would work for maintenance," Herb continued. "I've talked with the city fathers. Bet we can pretty much write our own ticket."

The airport had an interesting history. The city of Coeur d'Alene purchased the land in 1918, making it the first municipally owned airport in the U.S. After a few more minutes of frenzied discussion, the big question came: "What do you think, Gladys?"

I thought for a minute and replied, "Herb's the one who's there. Tell him to do what he think's best." I said.

"Make the deal, then," Gwin told Herb. "Explain the improvements the city will need to do, so we'll comply with the CAA requirements. You're gonna need to find a place to house and feed the students."

Unfortunately, Herb found the city unable to finance any of the necessities—a large storage hangar, water main, office building, classroom, pilots' briefing room and telephone—since the Depression had hit Kootenai County harder than any county in Idaho. But the city did agree to a liberal contract if Buroker-Hicks put in the improvements. January 26, 1942, Buroker-Hicks signed a lease for Weeks Field.

Herb scouted the town for quarters. In no time he rented an empty building on the southwest corner of Appleway and Government Way with Arnold's Auto Court lettered on the window. With the deals made, the real work began. Gwin ran the show in Pasco while Herb and I looked for a place to live. We checked into the Desert Hotel in Coeur d'Alene and then headed to Gridley Investment Company to meet Larry Cleveland who told us he would show available houses in the morning.

That night at dinner I said, "Herb, do you really think we should buy a place? What if we need to move again?"

"My dad told us kids never to rent if we could buy," Herb replied. "Paying rent is money down the drain."

It seemed a third of the houses in Coeur d'Alene had sale signs, and many were empty. By noon I had picked a small, two bedroom house with a full basement. "I want the house on 4th Street," I told Mr. Cleveland, but he kept showing us others. Finally I raised my voice a bit. "We don't need to look further. I want the white house on 4th Street."

Cleveland sighed and fessed up. "Actually that house is under

Arnold Auto Court on the southwest corner of Government Way and Appleway housed the St. Martins students in 1942.

Air view of Weeks Field - 1943.

a rental lease agreement, so I can't sell it." My disappointment was so evident, he added, "Let me talk with the tenants. Maybe they'll move if I can find another place they like."

Herb and I headed back to the Desert Hotel. Coeur d'Alene had really impressed me. The people we met treated us like old friends, and the town of 12,000 had no freeways. What a perfect place to set up business and raise a family.

Mr. Cleveland called the next morning with good news. The tenants had agreed to move. When we arrived back in Olympia, Gwin and Viv didn't comment about our purchase, but their expressions told us we were crazy. Our employees spoke right up. "Are you nuts? You could be moving again in a month." They snickered even more when they arrived in Coeur d'Alene to all the empty rentals. Once in a while, though, you get lucky which happened in our case.

Work began on Farragut Naval Base three months later. Situated twenty miles north of town on enormous Lake Pend Oreille, the base would soon house more people than the largest city in northern Idaho. Overnight military personnel would flood Coeur d'Alene and rent skyrocket. By the time the Navy moved in boot camp trainees, a house couldn't be had.

With Herb cracking the whip, St. Martin's yellow school bus, followed by our maintenance truck and trailer, caravaned from Pasco to Weeks Field. Meanwhile I needed to transport the aircraft. Four J3 Cubs in Pasco, plus our two planes at Olympia Airport, had to be flown to Coeur d'Alene. We decided I should take one student to Olympia, get permission from the military to fly our aircraft out of the defense zone, stop in Pasco to pick up the Cubs flown by four more students, and ferry to Coeur d'Alene. I picked the most promising pilots although none had cross-country flying experience or used an aviation chart. I doubt they had even seen one.

Chuck Sutherland, the most experienced of the group, road the bus with me to Olympia. Weather control told us we couldn't cross the Cascades because of low-cloud ceiling. After long hours confined in the hangar, I finally convinced the military to let us fly south to the Columbia River, then east through the gorge to the Dalles, OR. Actually, I think they were glad to get rid of us. Once personnel had alerted all area installations of our route and time schedule, we took off, arriving in Pasco by dark.

The next morning I struggled to hide my nervousness as I gathered my five students for a briefing. "Fly one behind the other, keeping the plane ahead in sight. The weather's not great, but ceiling and visibility meet CAA requirements. Any questions?" The boys looked as excited as a bunch of eight year olds headed to a carnival. I knew better. "Okay, let's go," I said.

About every fifteen minutes I would make a 90 degree turn to count the cubs. After the third time, I relaxed but not for long. The further east we got, the higher the terrain climbed and the lower the cloud ceiling dropped. To my horror, a smattering of snowflakes started sticking to my windshield. According to the chart- and I had the only chart- we should be nearing Ritzville. Past the halfway mark on fuel, I knew we couldn't turn back.

"It's just a little snow flurry," I told myself, but the farther we flew, the heavier it fell. I soon realized the visibility in the snow storms was far worse than in the rain storms—like being wrapped in cotton. If I dropped below 500 feet, I could see straight down. That was it.

I was desperate for a suitable place to land when I spotted Sprague Lake and then an open field at the north end. "This is it," I told myself. I turned 360 degrees, the cubs following like a brood of ducklings. That's when I spotted cottonwoods littering the approach end of the field. But we were out of options. .

I maneuvered over the trees and down into the snowy field, hopping out to guide in each pilot. If his approach looked shaky, I'd wave him off; if it looked good, I'd signal a landing. Two boys made it down on their first try, but the others took an eternity, or so it seemed, to work around the trees. Once down, they piled out.

"You guys did great!" I said, shaking each hand. "You followed instructions perfectly." They strutted around like banty roosters, laughing and punching each other, but I felt like collapsing. We positioned the planes the best we could to protect them from the weather, then headed south toward a light. As I hoped, the farmer who owned this property lived close by.

Painfully aware of how strange we must look in our snow-covered flight gear, I knocked on the farmhouse door. "May I use your phone?" I asked the middle-aged woman who answered. "We were flying to Coeur d'Alene but were forced down by the storm." Puzzled, she looked out her window but couldn't see a thing. She eyeballed me again. I wouldn't blame her had she slammed the door in my face. "I'll let you use the phone, but they stay outside," she said in a hard voice, pointing to the boys. I dialed with shaky fingers while my hostess watched every move. "Gwin," I tried to sound calm when he answered. "The snow forced us down just north of Sprague Lake."

"Is everyone all right?" he asked.

"We're fine, but we need you to come get us," I answered.

"Herb called half hour ago from Harrington," Gwin told me. "He went down too. He's worried sick." Somehow hearing Herb's name calmed me down a little.

"Don't worry, Gladys," Gwin said. "The station wagon's ready to go. We'll leave soon as we locate some tie-downs for the cubs."

When I hung up, the lady grabbed my arm. "You poor thing," she said, leading me to a chair by the fireplace. She called in the boys, fed us coffee and sugar cookies, and plied us with questions.

"You're not going to believe this," she laughed when her shocked husband walked in the door a bit later. She tried to explain but kept tripping over her words. The more she talked, the more suspicious he got, especially when he walked to the window and couldn't see a thing.

Thank goodness our mechanic arrived shortly after, asking the boys to unload the equipment and help carry it to the airplanes. Our host tagged along. When they got back to the house, the excited farmer told his wife, "Guess what!. There really is six airplanes down there!"

Chapter 11: Trials and Tribulations of War

BAD NEWS FOR DICTATORS
It's fighting planes and bombers...together with the skill
of the U.S. Navy pilots that are spelling VICTORY in countless air battles over the seas today. Aircraft plants throughout the nation are working at breakneck speeds to produce thousands upon thousands of the world's finest planes so that our air force can maintain supremacy in the skies.

<u>We are happy to be able to do our part</u> in providing pilots to fly in Uncle Sam's great air forces and we wish to commend these young men most highly for their cooperative spirit and outstanding sincerity in the work they are doing for their country.

Buroker/Hicks advertisement in
Coeur d'Alene Press on Navy Day

Exhausted, I fell asleep riding back to Coeur d'Alene. When we pulled into Weeks Field, Herb met the car, folding me in his arms. "Don't scare me like that, Peach," he whispered. "I'd die without you." Once the storm passed four days later, Herb took a crew of experienced pilots back to Sprague Lake to retrieve the planes.

Meanwhile, we got back to work, trying hard to keep our chins up. Leaving Olympia Airport only two months before for the sod runway at Weeks Field seemed worse than trading a Bentley for a sway-backed horse. Most pilots rated Olympia

Airport the best in the Pacific Northwest; they didn't know Weeks existed. It would take nearly $26,000 and lots of sweat to whip the field into shape.

Just when we needed supplies the most, rationing took effect. The psychological impact caused by this sudden loss of freedom devastated everyone at first. We were thankful war-related activities guaranteed us enough gas to get back and forth to work, though I rode my bike when I could. Food was rationed, too, with sugar falling in approximately the same category as solid gold. As war contractors we lucked out again since we fed military students, even managing a batch of chocolate chip cookies now and then (for which I still feel guilty fifty years later).

In spite of such overwhelming changes, we resolved to become operational in record time. With the U. S. embroiled in war, the military took over all civilian pilot training. In early spring of 1942, the War Training Service (WTS) notified us that our Civilian Pilot Training Program contract would terminate when St. Martin's and North Idaho Junior College's students completed the course. We really had to scramble to bring the facility into line with CAA requirements while completing that group's training. We knew the new War Training Service recruits were pouring in.

It was a sad day when the St. Martins school bus pulled out of Weeks Field, sending our beloved

Father Gerald of St. Martins College, Lacey, WA.

Father Gerald back to Lacey, WA. About the time St. Martins was leaving, North Idaho Junior College, which occupied the second and third floors of City Hall, was entering the WTS's Pilot Training Program, providing ground school instruction for army or navy recruits assigned to Buroker/Hicks Flying Service.

We needed a place to house all these students. I don't know where Herb and Gwin got the lead on the Civilian Conservation Corps (CCC) barracks at Beauty Bay on Lake Coeur d'Alene, but we figured they'd do fine for offices and classrooms. Since we contracted with the government (who owned the buildings), we got them for free. Gwin hired Lafferty Transportation to float the barracks to the Coeur d'Alene city dock where the boys loaded them on a flat bed truck and hauled them to Weeks.

Not only did we need to plan for crowds on the ground that summer but for congestion in the air as well. Our chief pilot, Howard "Brick" Wellman asked several flight instructors—Pete Peterson, Pat O'Grady and me— to establish some safety rules. He spread a U.S. Forest Service map on a table in the flight office. "We need specific areas assigned to each primary and secondary instructor," he said. "What are your suggestions?"

Even after looking the map over and agreeing to divide the Rathdrum Prairie six ways, we still needed more flight space. I thought about it for a minute. "Since secondary training requires flying at a higher altitude than primary," I said, "wouldn't it be

24 Navy and 10 Army students arrive at Weeks Field - 1942.

114

safe to use the treed area north of Lone Mountain and south of Athol? That way the prairie could be used exclusively for primary." The others agreed, and the plan worked well.

By mid-1943 our flight program would grow to thirty-eight flight instructors and two hundred students. Just transporting them to Weeks each day would pose a challenge. Early on, Brick used station wagons, but as the WTS brought in more recruits, we loaded them in side-rail trucks like a bunch of cattle. When I look at their photos now, I'm reminded of Jews being hauled to concentration camps.

When temperatures hit the 80's and 90's that summer, teaching became a challenge. Somehow we had to coax a fifty horsepower Cub, loaded with parachuted human cargo, to 5,300 feet above sea-level in order to teach spins. If we were lucky enough to spot a dust devil (updraft), we could lift like an elevator. More often, we ran the throttle full forward for half an hour to get to altitude, working those little Cubs pretty hard.

Gladys and students at Weeks Field classroom - 1942.

While the flight program gained momentum, Herb concentrated on renovating Week's only hangar. He updated the electrical wiring, installed an oil heating system, and hired workers to lay the water main from the field to Coeur d'Alene city limits at Appleway. The work pace at this point seemed frantic. Once he got the shop operational, Herb did the impossible, maintaining forty seven aircraft and supervising up to twenty five mechanics. In spite of the enormous job, airplanes rarely got grounded for more than twelve hours, earning Herb the reputation as the best aircraft mechanic in the Pacific Northwest.

Herb cut our "down time" by assembling day and night crews of crack mechanics. At the day's end, he asked each instructor to submit a squawk sheet, listing maintenance and repair needs for the airplane flown that day, so by morning the work would be

Transporting students from barracks
at North Idaho College to
Coeur d'Alene Air Terminal - 1943.

Instructors Pat O'Grady and
Howard (Pete) Peterson.

done. In case of emergencies, Herb kept spare engines on hand for overnight replacement. The day crew worked hard, too, on the more time-consuming overhauls and structural jobs.

Herb didn't get much sleep, hitting the airport by six a.m. to check the night repairs. If the mechanics were stumped by a stubborn problem, he'd put them on another job and take over. Nearly always the plane in question taxied onto the flight line by eight.

After breakfast, he'd review the work-in-progress and ask his clerk to order parts, a tough job since aircraft wrecking yards didn't exist and the war had slowed down supply lines. Yet Herb, quick to isolate an engine's problem, usually managed to find a quick remedy by scavenging every nook and cranny in the Northwest. He never, ever forgot wrecked planes stashed in people's back yards.

By fall we had met all the CAA requirements and even completed the framework for a new hangar, though it still had no roof. Herb for the first time in months was able to let-up a bit. In the mood for entertainment, he invited several mechanics and instructors to go hunting, his all-time favorite activity next to fishing. I stayed behind with Sally. Several days later the group returned toward evening, dying to show-off their prizes. Leave it to Herb to outdo the rest.

The next morning, employees pulling into Weeks were greeted by an remarkable sight. A large buck deer holding a rifle sat upright in the Ercoupe. Draped over the wing lay my clown-of-a-husband with ropes tying him down and his tongue hanging out. I guess in this case, the deer got his man.

It's a good thing we accomplished so much that first summer because we were unprepared for Idaho winters—especially this one. The first snow fell around Thanksgiving with temperatures dropping below 32 degrees and snow piling up. Herb found a local to plow the runway which worked fine for a while, but as snow deepened, the grader couldn't keep up. Gwin solved the problem by hiring the State of Idaho's rotor plow to blow the

Herb Buroker on wing of Ercoupe. "Buck deer gets his man."

snow to one side. We had to make-do with that. Takeoffs and landings became treacherous when snow berms blocked our view of the runway from the flight office. Getting airplanes in and out was a nerve-wracking process.

Then came the deep-freeze. Temperatures dropped to 35 below zero, forcing Herb to work round-the-clock thawing pipes to keep heating systems operational. After the initial cold snap, a day over fifteen degrees was rare. Our biggest headache was just getting off the ground. If the temperature dropped around ten, the airplanes (which sat outside) wouldn't start. Herb bought space heaters. Every morning the crew plugged them in with long electric cords, aiming the heat toward the engines and draping canvas over the cowlings to contain it. Because of fire hazard, someone had to monitor the heaters, a frustrating waste of man hours. As an alternative we tried draining the oil after the last flight, then heating and replacing it the next morning. That worked but took too much time.

Starting the engines was only part of the problem. Frost and snow would build on the airplane wings, fuselage, tail surfaces

Gladys getting ready to fly with Ensign Ed Norberg in the Timm Aerocraft.

and prop. To lift properly, the plane needed to be clean, forcing pilots to report at least an hour before flight to help the mechanics ready the planes. Starting at the fuselage with one person in front of the wing and another in back, the team would drag a rope back and forth, working out to the tip. Then with a cloth they would wipe down the fuselage, tail and prop.

Once airborne, everyone froze. Even in the cabin aircraft, heaters didn't do well. The Cub's heating system ran a tube at foot level from the exhaust through the fire wall into the front seat where instructors sat. Students in the back seat were out of luck. The open-cockpit airplanes challenged even the toughest. As the WTS needed us to train year round, it issued sheepskin flight gear to pilots. The pants zipped together from front to back with suspenders hitching them up. The jacket zipped up the front, with a flap over the zipper to block the wind. Sheep-lined boots, gloves and helmet topped off the outfit, turning us into adult-sized teddy bears.

The gear helped some but not enough. Except for take-offs and landings, most advanced flight maneuvers —spins, stalls, chandelles, and lazy eights—took place above 3,000 feet. Since the air cools two degrees for every thousand feet under standard conditions, the temperature was at least six degrees colder than on the ground, oftentimes more. Each flight lasted one hour. The students didn't notice the cold as much, but the instructors, who often had three flights in a row, walked like boards at the end of a shift. We complained, but we all survived.

Herb did a jig with spring break-up on Lake Coeur d'Alene sometime in April. My reaction was a bit more mild, but I sure looked forward to shirt- sleeve weather and fishing. We especially liked Kokanaee (Blue Back Salmon) and hoped to spend some time fishing Lake Pend Oreille.

With the snow gone, we finished our 50' x 100' hangar which soon sheltered 18 to 20 stacked planes, including the Piper Cubs and Taylorcrafts. To load the hangar tightly, Herb built a T-shaped dolly with three small wheels. The top of the T would hold the airplane wheels while mechanics maneuvered the tail into an upright position. Then they'd lift it from the dolly still holding the rear up until the nose touched padding on the floor. When the hangar was packed for the night, the planes looked like stacked cord wood.

That summer the WTS added night flying to the primary training program, a wrinkle we hadn't expected. Since most of our aircraft didn't come equipped, Herb ran them through the shop to install navigation lights wired to a battery. For runway lights, we loaded a pickup bed with kerosene lanterns. A half hour before dusk, the driver slowly steered along the runway's edge, and a crewman would drop a lantern every thirty feet or so, lining both sides with what looked like a string of illuminated pearls from the air. The morning crew, would follow the same route, retrieving the lanterns to trim wicks, clean globes and fill with kerosene.

Although we felt confident all contingencies had been covered for night flying, we could never have predicted one hazard. Students either trained at Weeks or at the Coeur d'Alene Air Terminal a few miles away. Neither field was fenced. Pat O'Grady, our youngest instructor at twenty, was soloing a student one night in the spring of '43. A talented pilot and promising

Piper J-5 after encounter with a horse during a night landing - 1943.

teacher, Pat was still wet-behind-the-ears in many ways. When Brick introduced us, I remember thinking, "This boy has a lot to learn." Although Pat looked all-man with his flaming red hair and ruddy complexion, his high-water plaid pants and wide eyes told us a bit about his maturity.

Pat stood on the runway this particular evening, watching a student fly his solo pattern and make landings in a Piper J5. Lining up with the runway and dropping smoothly for the third time, the student passed in and out of Pat's vision, nearly down and in perfect form. Then came a sickening crunch. Horrified, Pat dropped his clipboard and sprinted into the dark only to find the blood-spattered Piper upside down. Now out of his seat belt, the dazed student climbed onto the wing and staggered down its length, leaving tracks where he stepped through the fabric—crunch, crunch, crunch.

"Lay down," Pat shouted, helping the boy to the ground. Tearing off his shirt, Pat wiped blood from the student's face, arms, torso, and legs, feeling for cuts and broken bones but not finding a scratch. After a quick survey of the area, Pat solved the mystery. A farmer must have left a gate open, his unlucky horse winning a one-way ticket to horsey heaven. The rest of us thought it hilarious that Pat of all people had the misfortune to be teaching that night.

Pat had worked with us for a year by that time and had trained a lot of cadets and could fly like an ace. What he longed for was action. That summer he talked with army recruiters, and in November the U.S. Army Air Corps awarded him a direct commission. Pat quickly distinguished himself in the China-Burma Theater flying the "Hump" and numerous other military operations for which the Air Corps decorated him. He soon rose to Brigadier General. In November 1946, immediately after the war, Pat helped develop West Coast Airlines, the predecessor of Airwest, Hughes Air West and Republic. Thirty-six years later, Captain Pat O'Grady would retire from Republic Airlines number one in seniority out of 1,875 pilots.

The unfortunate student Pat had been instructing at Cd'A Air Terminal was one of a new group for Buroker/Hicks. While the new instructors concentrated on teaching primary and secondary classes, the more experienced, including Pat, Pete and I, took on a new assignment. The high brass at WTS had noted Buroker/Hicks' exemplary performance and thought of us immediately when they needed cross country instructors. They also liked the location of Weeks Field with open prairie to the west and high mountains to the east. Learning to fly in constantly changing wind currents and severe weather conditions was ideal for cadets entering the Ferry Command which flew supplies and soldiers in and out of the war zone.

"Expect forty seven cross-country students," the commander of Fort George Wright in Spokane told Gwin over the phone. They would begin arriving February 1943 with flight gear, parachutes and uniforms and would eventually turn our cross-country program into the largest west of the Mississippi. Most of the pilots we taught would be older men from all walks of life who wanted to help the war effort either as instructors or ferry pilots.

Herb's crews hastily installed the required radio equipment

Cross Country aircraft at Coeur d'Alene Air Terminal - 1934.

in the Gull-Winged Stinsons, Cabin Wacos and Fairchild 24's suitable for cross-country training. On each flight an instructor would work with three cadets on flying, navigation with charts and ground reference points, and radio operation. Since learning radio communication, in particular, was traumatic for students and even some instructors, the CAA built a traffic control tower on top of a Coeur d'Alene Air Terminal barrack. A cartoon I once saw pretty much summed up the pilots' problems. It showed an apprentice tower operator working the control panel with a bossy instructor hanging over his shoulder saying, "You're gonna hafta talk faster than that, or the pilots will understand you."

The top-speed delivery of technical language over less-than-perfect radio equipment made tower operators sound like they had mouths full of marbles, requiring a good set of ears and lots of practice on the part of pilots to understand. If students would have just radioed in, "I'm a student and can't understand your instructions," most operators would have gladly helped out (I have used this trick more than once at unfamiliar, high traffic airports). Most students, unfortunately, won't admit they are students.

Compared to radio communication, teaching flying seemed much easier. We used both Stinson Reliants and Fairchild 24's, the Fairchilds ranking heads above in my mind. A four-place cabin, high-wing monoplane, the Fairchild was powered by a 165 hp Warner engine—a taildragger with stick control. Like most taildraggers, it was intended for a sod runway which made it a bit touchy on the Coeur d'Alene Terminal's hard surface. In the air, though, it responded to the slightest pressure on the controls. I could literally fly it with my little finger, especially the Fairchild the military had requisitioned from Edgar Bergan.

We instructors planned three hour, triangular flights in these planes, so the cadet's assignment could rotate with each leg of the trip: first flying, then navigation, then radio communication. Our trips varied depending on the weather, but we tried to see that every student experienced different terrain and weather conditions. I frequently scheduled my flight plan to Missoula, Twin Falls, Boise, or to Pendleton, Yakima, Wenatchee and home. Even though I worked every angle to stay on schedule and get home to Herb and Sally, I spent more nights in strange airports waiting out bad weather than I care to remember. In our business, especially during the war, there was no such thing as an eight hour day.

My morning began at six a.m. with an alarm that would wake the dead. After bathing, dressing in military-issue slacks and blouse, and gobbling down scrambled eggs on toast, I'd give Christine, our babysitter, instructions for the day. Sally, tightly clutching her "teddy," would pad behind me to the door in her pajamas for a big good-bye hug and kiss. Mounting my bike propped against the garage, I'd pedal to the airport, hoping to catch Herb for a morning kiss as he headed to the restaurant for breakfast.

When I walked into the office, I'd pick up my flight schedule from Brick. A typical day might be training six cross country students with the first flight, leaving at 8 a.m. to Walla Walla, Yakima and back to Coeur d'Alene and the second, starting at 1:00 to Pendleton, Wenatchee and back. During the thirty to forty five minutes between the first and second flights, I'd grab a sandwich and catch my breath. Preparing for class seemed impossible, so while airborne, I'd sneak a few minutes to scribble out students' assignments for their next flight. If all went well, I'd be home for dinner and an evening with Sally.

Herb and I managed to get home less and less often as the war progressed. The trouble was that the military desperately needed pilots. For weeks on end, it seemed, Herb and I would work seven days a week, twelve hours or more a day. Since we both thrived under pressure, I thought we could handle it just fine. Looking back, I see I had on blinders.

The first headache hit one day, shortly after we arrived in Coeur d'Alene. Herb drove me home and put me to bed where the black cloud of pain blinded me and emptied my stomach for nearly forty-eight hours. Too weak to stand for several days after, I finally went to the doctor. "That's a migraine, my dear," he told me. "The best I can do is give you shots when they come on." The shots dulled the pain, but sometimes I'd lay in bed for days.

The long hours, stress of leaving Sally, and fear for my students' safety brought on these demons. During one cross country trip in 1943, I remember how tense things could get. Three students and I were nearing Pendleton in a Fairchild 24 when our first tank ran dry. The student at the controls switched tanks but nothing happened. "What do I do now?" he asked, his voice a little shaky.

"Guess we land," I replied. "Tighten your seat belts."

I spotted a stubble field below that looked promising. (Thank goodness the wheat has been cut). Taking the controls, I calmly instructed the now-silent students on how to land aircraft in unfamiliar terrain under adverse circumstances. (Dear lord, let me pull this off). The ground came up fast, but I managed a passable landing, although we bounced hard coasting to a stop.

"Wow!" one student laughed. "That scared the bejesus out of me." The other two let out breaths like they'd held them for five minutes straight. "How do we get out of this?" they asked.

I told them I thought the engine had vapor locked. "We'll just have to wait a few minutes and see if she'll start." We all piled out and walked the field, planning our takeoff procedure. "This is a good experience," I told them. "A ferry pilot never knows where he might have to land." Fifteen minutes later I climbed back into the cockpit and pushed the starter. The Fairchild fired right up, her instruments working normally. After a bumpy takeoff, I resumed routine instruction, but the students couldn't seem to concentrate. (I couldn't blame them a bit). I bet the hangar stories really flew that night. I, for one, was just glad to be home with my family.

Unfortunately, home seemed more and more remote as the war progressed and the demand for more pilots became increasingly urgent. The Navy, facing an emergency shortage of flight instructors organized five advanced Civilian Pilot Training schools to help, one of which was Buroker/Hicks. It offered commissions to young men with 140 hours of civilian training who could meet other Navy requirements. They would complete several months of school at Weeks and then proceed as flight instructors to Navy training bases at New Orleans or Pensacola.

Somewhere around June, Brick asked me to prepare for these students slated to arrive in late 1943, eight or nine months after the cross country training had begun. This group's training in 220 horsepower aircraft included 72 hours ground school and 50 to 60 hours flight instruction. I set aside one hour per day to brush-up for an aerobatics flight test in an open cockpit UPF-7 WACO. The day I took my test I was pleased the CAA Inspector was none other than Lou Becker, who had been on the Spokane-to-Glacier Park motorcycle trip Madeline and I joined a few years before.

Once underway, I found the Navy's Flight Instructor Course the most relaxed teaching I'd ever done. The officers were experienced pilots, so we had a blast doing aerobatics. One day I faced a forced landing with Ensign J. G. Frisch who demonstrated flawless planning, timing and landing.

Navy students Gladys trained in an aerobatic instructor course. From left Ensigns Jim Longmuir, Jack Frisch, John Botsford, Alfred Fredekind and Ed Norberg - 1944.

I entered the training program with Buroker/Hicks to earn an instructor's ticket in early fall of '43. The Navy had signed on five of us as Navy ensigns, and we were to proceed to Dallas as flight instructors after completing more instruction in aerobatics.

Brick Wellman assigned Gladys Buroker as my instructor, and I shortly found she could fly anything with wings. I also knew as Herb Buroker's wife that she had extensive background in early private aviation, having barnstormed, doing wing walking and parachute jumps at county fairs. My esteem for Gladys grew as I flew with her.

One incident really sticks in my mind. We were on a final check ride in midwinter with about a foot of powder on the ground. We took off from Weeks Field and flew into the countryside where Gladys had me demonstrate and talk through all the various maneuvers such as emergency landings, aerobatics, etc.

Gladys then told me, "Do a three turn normal spin and recover within 10 degrees of your starting position." I lined up with a fence and pulled the Piper Cruiser into a stall and a left-turn spin. About a halfway into the second turn, the propeller stopped. I was a bit upset!

Gladys, what do I do now?"

She didn't bat an eye. "Well—there is an airport right under you.," she said. "Go ahead and land!" So there was. The county was in the process of building a new airport, and the runways—all five thousand two hundred and eight feet of them—were outlined in the snow below. I did manage a good approach and landing. The powder flew as we rolled to a stop.

Gladys just climbed out and spun the propeller. The engine started, and we flew back to Weeks Field without further incident. Cool, calm, Gladys!

I went on to complete the Navy's Flight Instructor course and became a Naval aviator during the rest of World War II.

While I taught aerobatics and cross country that summer, Herb and Gwin began planning for the next bout of cold. Having learned a valuable lesson about nasty winters, we decided, after some conversation, to buy airplane skis rather than pay someone to plow runways. We could save money while increasing safety during take-off and landings. Forced landing on skis could also cause less damage. Experience had taught us wheels stop suddenly when they sink into the snow, flipping the plane with the forward momentum. In most cases the pilot walks away, unless he unbuckles his seat belt and drops on his head. The plane, though, takes a beating.

With the first good snow, we couldn't wait to try our new skis, both metal and wood. (We actually took one WTS class from start to finish on skis.) The older wood models turned out to be better performers under all snow conditions. The metal skis in temperatures slightly below or above 32 would freeze solid to snow. To break a plane loose, assistants would need to rock each wing back and forth while the pilot applied power. Once loose, the pilot couldn't stop, or the skis would again freeze immediately to the snow.

Piper J-3 on skis over Hayden Lake - Coeur d'Alene, ID.

Another challenge with skis was no brakes—whoo-ee-ee! The boys would taxi our snow-covered runway like a ski slope. We liked powder the best. Even if we put down incorrectly in a cross wind, it felt like landing on a feather bed—talk about fun! But with packed snow, handling became more difficult. On ice the rudder provides the only control, yet one needs speed before the rudder works. Takeoffs in particular could be wild. Quite often on the ground we had to push the airplane because we just couldn't taxi. The gas pump, surrounded by an ice-slick, needed extra hands to keep traffic moving.

We didn't have much time for Christmas celebrations with our frantic work pace. Then one Sunday morning the CAA-WTS dispatched a telegram to Buroker-Hicks Flying Service stating all WTS training activities would end effective that day, January 16, 1944. In less than twenty four hours our business would return to commercial activities as governed by wartime regulations.

Gwin called together the entire staff at a 1:00 meeting and relayed the news. "What'll we do about airplanes tied down at the Air Terminal?" someone asked.

"They need to be brought back here." he said. "You instructors wanna go over and fly 'em back?" We made a beeline for the two station wagons and piled in two deep. All the wild oats we had stored during the war sprouted that day in a joyous free-for-all. Guys sprinted to the nearest airplanes, fired them up with no safety checks, and treated onlookers to an incredible air show—slow rolls on takeoff, incredible loops and dives. It's a wonder no one collided.

I picked out a Stinson and headed south toward the college. Circling frozen Lake Coeur d'Alene, I came in low, tipping my wings at the students who, now quartered there, burst from barracks like bees from a hive; they couldn't believe I would flaunt CAA codes. It was so much fun, I buzzed them again. Too bad a military officer watched my second pass and wrote down my plane's number.

Not quite done, I flew over downtown, then hooked a left on Fourth so low I could practically pinch mail from the mailboxes. Back at Weeks I tied down the Stinson and quietly joined Herb and Gwin, both pretty upset by the shenanigans. After everyone had landed, laughing and beating each other on the backs, Gwin came out of the office. "Who was flying the NC34605?" he asked.

Everyone looked at each other, but no one said a word. I realized in a flash of embarrassment I was in trouble. Clamping my mouth shut, I figured the commotion would soon die down. The next day Willson Gillis, the local CAA inspector paid us a visit. He'd received a complaint, he said, and expected to get to the bottom of it. For six weeks he dogged us, asking the same questions over and over. Finally, I couldn't take it.

"You're not gonna give up till you get a license!" I said. "I was flying the airplane. Take mine—I won't be needing it anyway."

"Oh no, Gladys," he said, looking around for help. "I know you wouldn't do anything like that!" He couldn't get to his car fast enough.

That night in bed Herb read to me from an Earl Stanley Garner novel while Sally slept soundly between us. My attention drifted from his words as I thought of the future. Finally—at last—we could fish, go camping to Upper Priest, or even spend a day at the beach with Sally.

Chapter 12: Post War and Disaster

The next morning dawned clear and cold, the branches of the ice-covered maple out my kitchen window shimmering as I made a pot of coffee and sat down to read the *Coeur d'Alene Press*. The headlines announced the Allies were pushing back the enemy, the Japanese were on the run, and the troops would soon be home. A few minutes later Herb poured himself a cup and joined me at the table.

Almost overnight, it seemed, we were back where we started. Already Herb and Gwin had agreed to liquidate Buroker/Hicks once our contracts with the War Training Service were completed. Gwin, always the promotor, wanted to start a passenger airline in Lewiston, but we just didn't have that much energy.

After a few sleepless nights, we decided to stay at Weeks Field under a new business name, Aviation Industries, Inc., with Herb and myself working as instructors, mechanics, and pilots-for-hire. We needn't have worried about getting business. In a few short months our days stretched long as we gave passenger rides and arranged charter flights, taught students, and flew game counting/salt drop runs for the U.S. Forest Service.

The nation's fascination with war pilots and their adventures left lots of people just itching to fly. Though our Piper J5s' seventy-five-hp engines performed badly at Coeur d'Alene's elevation, we used them anyway for passenger rides. I don't recall ever getting higher than eight hundred feet when I flew two passengers from Weeks Field to scenic Tubbs Hill and back.

While I generally handled the passenger flights, Herb kept busy, early on, getting WTS aircraft ready to sell. The government gave previous owners of these aircraft the chance to repurchase them at reduced prices. If the owners did not want the planes (which was often the case), then Herb placed them for sale with the Defense Plant Corporation who disposed of government-owned aircraft.

These jobs brought in money, but we needed more predictable income. Thank goodness opportunity came knocking. Enlisted men, pouring back into the states, required vocational training, so the Veterans Administration notified all flight schools they could contract for veteran flight training, provided the schools ran CAA-approved operations and could supply acceptable curriculums. Up past midnight for several weeks, I mapped out a program for private, commercial and flight instructor courses, then packed my bags and took a train to Boise to negotiate with the V.A. I came home with good news for Herb—we'd netted a lucrative contract.

We needed to hire several instructors, but our former employees had left. Luckily we knew of several local army and navy pilots who needed very little tutoring to pass the CAA's test for an instructor's rating. Deciding to train them ourselves, Herb and I signed on Herb Munro, Joe Westover, Clay Henley and my brother, Cal Dawson.

Ten years younger than I, Cal would always be my baby brother. I still remember the terrified little boy hiding behind Mom's skirts whenever Dad turned into the driveway. Making up my mind early on to take Cal under my wing, I figured "Why not?" when he asked me to teach him to fly. With a pilot's license he could earn a living. The summer of 1942, just six months after Pearl Harbor, I invited Cal, then a junior in high school, to Coeur d'Alene. He had grown into a man overnight, it seemed, with a small, muscular frame, dark steady eyes and a heartwarming smile—the kind of kid who didn't know a stranger. Even with my backbreaking schedule, I took Cal out each morning for lessons. He caught on almost immediately, soloing in two and a half hours. After graduating from high school that next spring, Cal enlisted in the Army Air Corps and distinguished himself as a fighter pilot which gave him most of the qualifications we needed for a flight instructor.

I wasn't so sure about Clay Henley, who couldn't have been more handsome had he walked off a Hollywood set. He favored Clark Gable's good looks, but Clay was the real thing: a rebel, a charmer, definitely one-of-a-kind. When we first climbed into a cockpit, Clay seemed a little too cocky for my taste. Deciding he just didn't like women telling him what to do, I purposely assigned him a dog (an underpowered, rough-handling airplane) for training and later for his CAA flight test.

When he returned, certificate in hand, he strode angrily up to me. "You gave me that dog on purpose, didn't you?"

"Yes, I did," I said with a little grin. "I couldn't tell if you disliked flying with me, or you just wanted to prove you could fly."

He just stared at me for a minute. "You're wrong on the first count-I did like flying with you. But you're right on the second—I can fly anything." I watched Clay from that day until his death in 1977. In my opinion, he was right.

As if I didn't have enough to do, the CAA appointed me flight examiner for private and commercial applicants for both land and sea planes. Herb and I got a good laugh over that. Only a few months before, I thought the CAA officials might yank my license for buzzing the students' barracks; now I worked for them.

The timing couldn't have been worse for me to come down with a rotten case of the flu that fall. Unable to shake it, I visited our family doctor who didn't need a rabbit to tell me I was pregnant and due in May. What a shock! But the more I thought about it, the more excited I got. What a perfect way to celebrate my thirty-ninth year and the end of the war. I found Herb a few minutes later bent over an engine. "Guess what," I said.

"What," he answered, clearly more interested in the engine than in what I had to say.

"I'm not sick; I'm pregnant." The look on his greasy face couldn't have been more comical.

"You're what?" He grabbed my hands and danced me in circles. That night Herb treated me to the most elegant dinner we'd had since the war started. Too bad my morning sickness extended into the evening.

Salt drop for Forest Service with Stinson, Bitterroot Range.

Once the morning sickness passed, I actually felt better than I had in ages. While I swelled up like a balloon that winter, business boomed. So many inquiries about our program had come from the St. Maries area, thirty miles to the south, we decided to lease the St. Maries Airport and set up a satellite operation with Clay Henley in charge. As I flew each week to St. Maries to do the books, Lake Coeur d'Alene's bays and outlets became as familiar as the fingers on my hands. To my delight elk herds and coyotes (for whom the State of Idaho paid bounties) stood out in the snow. When I spotted them, I'd dip down for a closer look and follow them zigzagging through the white terrain.

It was the winter of 1947-48 that Floyd Runge and John Ruthven decided to help the farmers of Rathdrum Prairie by eliminating a few coyotes. Taking off in the ski-equipped Piper J-5, they returned about an hour later with evidence to collect their bounty. I'm sure it had nothing to do with the fact that they loved to hunt and fly.

One day the weather seemed questionable as I flew to the St. Maries office. An hour later I glanced up from my desk to see a skiff of snow drifting into the window and decided to leave early—just to be safe. Clay caught me on the way out. "Mind waitin' a bit?" he asked. "I'd like to catch a ride."

"No problem," I answered, even though a nasty storm seemed in the making. By the time our cub lifted off an hour later, the snow was falling hard. Following the St. Joe River to the Coeur d'Alene Lake and then down the east shoreline toward Coeur d'Alene, I noticed snow blanketing the frozen lake. Visibility got worse and worse—then white out.

"Clay can you see anything?" I asked. "Looks like I'm gonna have to land." He just shook his head.

" Wanna take over?" I added.

"You're doing fine," he answered. Throttling back, I held a northerly heading, hoping to keep us over the lake. The altimeter indicated 500 feet and falling. Feeling blindfolded, I added a little power while holding the airplane in landing configuration

Floyd Runge and John Ruthven following a successful coyote hunt on the Rathdrum Prairie.

until with slight bump we touched down as easily as landing on a field of cotton.

"Couldn't have done better myself," Clay said with a grin as we coasted to a stop. Though he acted calm, I know Clay followed my every move on the controls.

We figured we couldn't be far from the land, so I taxied slowly in an easterly direction until the shoreline, cupped against a steep bank, came into focus about ten minutes later. Pulling the airplane onto the shore, we battened it down as best we could, hoping the little bay we wandered into would shelter our cub. We climbed the bank and fought our way through snow-laden brush to the road, then decided to double back toward Harrison which we figured we had already passed. Taking a deep breath, I pulled my coat tighter around my protruding stomach and headed into the blizzard with Clay.

The welcome sound of a car plowing through the snow roused us from our solitary thoughts. Flapping our arms, we no doubt startled the driver who stopped and rolled down his window. "Hi!" Clay said walking to the car. Can you tell us where we are?"

"About four miles north of Harrison," the driver answered with a funny look on his face. "Whatcha doin' out here?"

We both started talking, but he stopped us. "Jump in. Looks like you need a ride, and I want to get home before this socks in." Clay answered his questions while I dripped all over the back seat. Twenty minutes later he dropped us at the Harrison Hotel.

The first thing I did was call Herb as I knew he would be worrying. "Stay overnight at the hotel," he told me. It's not safe on that road."

"Okay. I'll call ya in the morning."

Exhausted and still cold, I grabbed a ham and cheese sandwich with Clay and then escaped to my room for a hot bath and bed, relishing their warmth and safety. The next morning I awoke to the baby kicking as if to say, "Get up!" I pulled back the white curtains covering the hotel window to a crystal blue sky and snowy landscape that reminded me of Christmas cards I'd sent out in December. After breakfast Clay and I hitched a ride to the airplane, fired her up after brushing off the snow, and landed safely in Coeur d'Alene a few minutes later.

May 15, 1945
Mr. and Mrs. H. A. Buroker, Co-Partnership
Announcing—Second Model, with Approved
Type Certificate, Called
Linda Lee

Specifications
Same, general, lines as 1940 product,
retaining two place open cockpit
Gross weight 8 lbs. 3 1-2 ozs.:
tear drop designed fuselage, pug nose, two blisters on
forward portion, special designed empennage
muffler on exhaust,
color ruddy pink hand rubbed finish, covering best-grade
outing flannel obtainable, due to wartime restrictions.

We Invite Your Inspection and Approval at
Buroker Residence, 1522 4th Street
Coeur d'Alene, Idaho

Winter passed. With the lilacs came the baby, Linda Lee, who I delivered May 15, 1945, two weeks after quitting work. We loved her so much that Herb and I would quarrel good-naturedly over who got to change diapers and give her baths. Five-year-old Sally elbowed her way in too, wanting more than anything to hold her baby sister.

Time seemed to blur the next few years as it can with a new baby in the house. I will never forget, though, the first time the Union Oil Goodyear Blimp toured the Northwest, spending a few days at Weeks Field. The whole setup fascinated me, especially takeoffs and landings. A large ground crew held the buoyant monster to the ground with ropes. If even one rope was missed when the blimp came in, the pilot had to make a circle the size of a football field to come in for another try. Once tethered, the blimp wrestled the ropes while new passengers rushed to load. When ready, the captain signaled the crew to let go. Away they'd float, wallering around like a motorless boat adrift on the waves.

Except for little distractions liked this, Herb and I spent our time building the business. We spent plenty on advertising, trying to catch the public's eye.

We Will Teach You to Fly For. . . **$80**
"SURE—YOU CAN FLY! As Easy As Driving a Car"
Costs only $5.00 to start

Don't let the shopping gremlins get you—
GIVE FLIGHT LESSONS FOR CHRISTMAS.
$5—$10—$15
Certificates Available

Encouraged by the business these little blurbs brought in, Herb kept his eye open for new advertising schemes. One day Harry Minor, who managed the Wilma Theater, met Herb for coffee

Goodyear blimp giving rides at Weeks Field, Coeur d'Alene, ID - 1945.

and pie at O'Reilly's on the south end of Weeks' original hangar where they could watch air traffic and shoot the bull at the same time.

"Heard about *Blaze of Noon*?" Harry asked Herb.

"Can't say I have."

"It's about the adventures of a sky pioneer. I'm lookin' for some aviation memorabilia to put in the lobby. Could ya help me out?" By the time Harry stopped by my office to say good-bye, Herb had promised him we would not only outfit the lobby but hoist a real-live airplane onto the Wilma's marquee.

A wee bit concerned, I asked Herb at lunch, "What airplane did you have in mind?"

"The PA-11," he answered with his mouth full.

"But it's brand new! " We'd just received the Piper PA-11 (a streamlined J3 Cub) as a demonstrator.

"It won't get a scratch," Herb said, eyeing me. "What's the matter— don't you trust me?"

"Well, if anyone can do it, I guess it's you," I said into my plate. Once Herb got a notion like this, I knew he wouldn't be stopped.

The next day Herb hauled the Cub downtown to the Wilma. With a crowd gathered to watch, he somehow lifted it onto the marquee, so the nose hung just over the edge and the tail hiked vertically toward the sky.

Painted on its side was "Aviation Industries" with our phone number. Needless to say, motorists driving down main street couldn't miss the sight. Herb's idea generated numerous comments from the downtown merchants, but movie buffs flocked to the display as did reporters. And true to Herb's word, the cub returned to Weeks good as new.

We tried another advertising scheme when we became dealers for Ercoupes in 1945. "Why not display one at the Kootenai County Fair?" I asked Herb who thought it a great idea. Located close to Lake Coeur d'Alene, the fairgrounds had no facilities for landing, but Herb thought I could probably taxi the five miles

Herb Buroker and Harry Minor advertising the movie BLAZE OF NOON
with Piper PA11. Wilma Theater, Coeur d'Alene, ID - 1945.

if we handled it right. The day of the fair, I started about 6:00 a.m. with Herb leading in a car, so he could signal oncoming traffic to pull off the road. I taxied down Highway 95 from Weeks Field to Appleway, turned left toward 15th, heading south on 15th to Sherman Avenue, turned right on Sherman to 7th, and finally angled left to the fairground building. The sight of an airplane hogging the road must have seemed pretty strange from a driver's perspective—cars pulled off the road, and people ran out of their houses to get a good look. It's hard to believe we did that; life was so simple back then.

Even with the slower pace, things could get sticky at Weeks Field. In fact, the nearest I came to crashing evolved from a seemingly simple event. A student called from Hayden Lake, telling us engine trouble forced him down in a meadow near the east end. This surprised us as Hayden was not a practice area. "He was probably doin' a little sightseeing," I told Herb as everyone climbed into the truck. We found him half an hour later. The plane's left wing, landing gear and propeller had been damaged, but the engine seemed okay.

Ercoupe on way to Fair on 15th Street - 1946.

Ercoupe now in town on Sherman Ave. - 1946.

After some head scratching, Herb decided to make temporary repairs in the field, so we could fly the cub to the airport for major surgery. While Herb worked, I walked the short, bumpy meadow, realizing takeoff would be hazardous. I noticed Herb huddled with the guys as I strolled back. He turned to me. "I've talked it over with the fellas. We agree you should fly out."

"Why me?" I asked, flabbergasted.

"I think the guys are all too heavy."

I can't say I was excited about the prospect but decided I'd risk it. Herb drained all the gas, then put back four gallons after which he took out the cushions, emptied the baggage compartment, and removed the battery and landing light used for night flying. I planned to take off early the next morning when the cool air would give better lift.

The grass dripped with dew as we pulled the stripped cub far back into the meadow. I got in, and Herb propped the plane. While holding the brakes to allow the oil temperature to rise, I checked the mags and carburetor heat. Then opening the throttle, I released the brakes and held my breath.

Rather than picking up speed, the little cub bounced like a bronco over the potholes and weeds. "Should I stop?" I asked myself near panic. Finally the tail lifted, and by holding it low, I had better control. Water was coming too fast, but I was almost up. Hitting a bump, the plane lifted-then dropped back to the

Piper J-5 Gladys flew out after repairs in the field.

ground—too late to abort. "This is it," I thought "I'm gonna crash."

Barely above stall speed, the cub finally lifted at the water's edge, and I gently relaxed the back-pressure on the stick until it began to climb. Drenched with sweat, in spite of the cool air, I shivered all the way back to Weeks and wasn't too steady the rest of the day either. Herb and the guys congratulated me—"We knew you could do it." To this day I'm sure I'm the only one who realizes how close I came to injury or death.

This incident sobered me a lot. I always got lucky, it seemed, but how long could my luck hold out? Little did I know a mammoth disaster was in the making. Cal and Clay Henley, both intensely interested in aviation, decided to build an experimental airplane with Glenn Johnson, Clay's childhood friend, who joined them as chief designer and mechanic. Planning to enter their racer in the Goodyear Midget Trophy Race, the three worked every spare minute in Clay's backyard garage. After 2,500 hours of sweat and toil, they had the Pistol Ball, as the boys dubbed her, ready to test fly. Eighteen feet long with an eighteen foot wing span, the tiny plane, powered by a Continental 85 horsepower engine, weighed only 520 pounds.

I watched at Weeks Field the first time she flew. With Cal at the controls, the Pistol lifted off like an awkward, little bird. Man was she fast as Cal flew her to Spokane and back with no problems. After a few more successful test flights, the trio headed to Cleveland for the September 4, 1948, race. Hoping for 195 mph, the guys were disappointed by the Pistol's qualifying speed of 142.343 mph. But Cal placed third in the semi-finals later that day, assuring the Pistol Ball a shot at the finals—or so he thought. During a down-wind landing (as ordered by the control tower), Cal lost control and ground looped, buckling the landing gear and damaging a wing tip. Since there was no way the team could finish repairs in time for the final race, they took the Pistol Ball apart and shipped her home by rail. Thrilled by their success, the three used her parts to start immediately on the next year's new, improved model.

Glen Johnson, Clay Henley and Cal Dawson with "Pistol Ball" they built for the Goodyear Trophy race in Cleveland.

By August of the next year the threesome completed their second racer, Clay's Pigeon. Early in the planning stage, Cal had told Clay and Glenn he wouldn't fly the Pigeon because he simply couldn't take a chance with his wife pregnant. This posed no problem—the fellows simply made the cockpit a little roomier to accommodate Clay's 6 foot 3 inch, 200 pound body. In the new design they also incorporated a controversial cantilever stabilizer (without external bracing). Herb, feeling they needed wire bracing, tried to discourage the idea. But nationally-known aeronautical engineer, Milt Chester, looked at the design and liked it. Since he was the CAA's chief regional engineer, the guys chose to take his advice.

Unlike the previous year, the test flights proved frustrating. A fuel line problem stymied the boys until someone found two drops of babbitt metal that had inadvertently dropped in the fuel line during construction. That problem solved, it was time to fly. To everyone's dismay, Clay couldn't cram himself into the cockpit. What could they do? The next day a critical test flight had been scheduled with the Spokane CAA who would clock the midget's speed. Cal agreed to fly the plane just this once. Excited, he called me that night, full of news and predictions. Smaller than the Pistol Ball, the Pigeon would be certain to fly faster. He was sure!

For some reason I tossed and turned all night. The next morning, I paced the flight office. "He'll be fine," I kept telling myself, but my gut told me something else. Unable to stand it another minute, I hopped in a cub and flew to the Terminal. I found Cal, cheerful as ever, doing his preflight check.

"I'm worried," I said, watching him go through the checklist.

"Come on, Sis," he said, grabbing me around the shoulder and squeezing. "You know if anything happened to me, I'd die happy." He kissed my cheek and gave me a smile that said, "I love ya, but I'm busy." Feeling overprotective, I headed back to Weeks—I had students to teach.

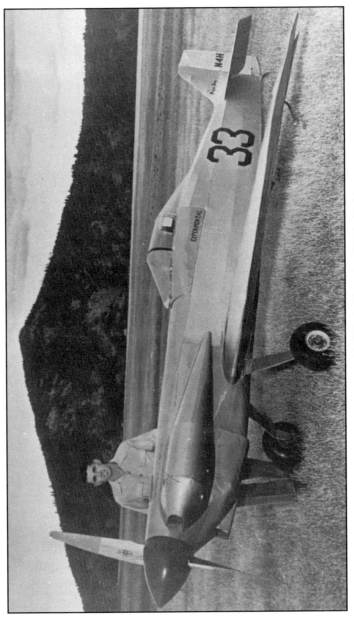

Cal Dawson with "Clay's Pigeon" at Weeks Field.

Cal took off thirty minutes later. The flight went beautifully, the Pigeon clocking speeds in excess of 160 mph. What happened next seemed unclear at first. A farmer plowing his field told authorities he saw the plane flying behind a national guard AT-6 (the CAA plane) when it "seemed to get caught in the backwash of the big plane, flipped, levelled off and then crashed into the ground." He also saw the pilot raise out of the cockpit, apparently trying to escape, before it hit.

Spokesman Review reporter, Birney Blair, had a much more accurate account. Assigned to cover the flight test, he was seated in the AT-6 flying right next to Cal. He said the midget was traveling about 160 mph when the horizontal stabilizer Herb had been worried about began flapping wildly. Within seconds it broke loose, and the plane took a nose dive, killing Cal instantly.

The phone call came shortly after. "The Pigeon crashed," Clay told me in a pained voice. "Cal's dead." Then he hung up.

I don't know who blamed himself more. I despaired in my darkest moments. Wasn't it I who taught Cal to fly? Herb felt he should have pushed more for a design change. Didn't he know the blasted thing wouldn't work? Clay knew he was to blame. Shouldn't he have sat in that cockpit instead of Cal? And then there were Cal's wife, Peggy, and six-month-old Judy. What would they do?

Cal's death took the shine off my love of flying. I felt tired and discouraged—I think Herb did too. Then another tragedy broadsided us the spring of 1950. We had brought the girls, then nine and four, to Weeks one nice evening after supper as Herb needed to repair the landing gear on a Piper Cub and I had some office work to do. Good at entertaining themselves, Sally and Linda took their dolls to the back of the hangar. While I talked with Sid, a flight instructor helping Herb, I could hear the girls chattering away while they changed diapers and gave bottles to their babies. "Time to get to work," I told Sid and headed for the office.

The guys, planning to weld, removed the cub's wheel, rested the axle on a dolly and rolled it near the hangar entrance as a safety precaution. Herb had barely started welding when strut fabric touching the hot metal tubing burst into flame. Sid grabbed the nearby fire extinguisher and doused it good.

"Let's roll it outside to finish," Herb said. Sid started pushing the dolly with Herb balancing the cub when the fabric flamed up again. "Damn," Herb yelled. "Get it out of here!" Sid pushed faster while Herb tried to contain the fire when suddenly the Cub slipped off the dolly. Frantic, they tried to muscle the plane out the door until the heat drove them off. Within seconds the plane exploded into flames.

Brilliant light flickered on a window, teasing my eyes away from my books. The first thought I registered was—FIRE!! The second—THE GIRLS!! In a panic I raced past Herb and Sid struggling with the Cub into the hangar already filled with smoke. The girls still sat on the concrete floor but both rubbed their burning eyes. "Give me your hands," I said, trying to stay calm. Linda jumped right up, but Sally dragged her feet. "But mom," I heard her say as I pulled them out the stock room door. "But mom!!"

Before I could get to the car, Sally jerked away and ran back toward the burning hangar. "Come back here, Sally," I screamed.

"I want my dolly," I heard her shout. Afraid to leave Linda alone, I picked her up and ran after Sally, but by the time I reached the hangar, Sally ran back out of the smoke, holding her doll by the hair.

Helpless, we sat on the runway and watched the destruction of our livelihood. The fire started at 8:00 p.m, and the fire engines arrived at 8:15. There was little they could do other than keep the fire contained. Gasoline in the planes, a quantity of solvent, and the highly explosive "dope" used to stiffen fabric, spread the blaze in great explosions. More than a dozen firemen and volunteers, who battled the fire for several hours, did manage to save the northwest corner of the building where the furnace stood and a quantity of coal was stored. They also prevented the flames from spreading to the large hangar to the north and the office building to the south.

"We're safe. Thank God we're safe." That's all Herb and I could think as we four snuggled, reading children's books late that night. But the blackened remains of the hangar made me cry the next day. Though all our work since 1941 seemed to have gone up in smoke, we halfheartedly picked up the pieces and continued business. The big hangar and flight office had escaped damage, and a blanket insurance policy owned by the City and Aviation Industries covered most losses. Unfortunately the damages and the location of Weeks Field got the city fathers to thinking. The next surprise would be the last straw.

Shortly after the fire, the City of Coeur d'Alene told us our lease would not be renewed in December. With Weeks Field hemmed in on three sides by a highway and housing areas, an expanding air field seemed illogical, especially with the Coeur d'Alene Terminal located only five miles to the north. Instead, we were told, the city had cut a deal with Kootenai County to develop Weeks into a fairground within the year.

Herb and I did a lot of talking about what to do. We discussed moving to the Coeur d'Alene Air Terminal, but that would mean starting all over. We had invested and lost money at Weeks and weren't too keen about repeating that, especially on property we didn't own. One evening we wound our way through the same conversation again. Herb was stretched out on the couch and I sat at the table, hashing over our options like dogs worrying a bone.

"Come here, Peach," Herb said. "You look so tired." He pulled me down beside him and started rubbing my shoulders. "Don't you think we've earned a rest? We've worked seven days a week for seventeen years. Let's just sell the planes and take it easy for a couple of years."

Chapter 13: Wolf Lodge

I'll never forget my shock. "What'll we do?" I asked.

"Let's sell the house and buy five acres out of town," he answered with a big grin. I'll build a shop for my tools and equipment, and you can grow a big garden." The idea seemed irresistible. . . nothing but quiet, peaceful farm-life with Herb and the kids. No pressure, no responsibility, no people.

"Okay," I answered. "Let's do it."

The more Herb and I looked at land, the more we realized we wanted space—lots of space. Our Realtor called one afternoon, telling Herb about a 140 acre piece of property thirteen miles east of town. Turning off Wolf Lodge Road the next day, we pulled into the prettiest spot this side of the Cascades. Two meadows, thick with Indian Paintbrush and Goldenrold, spread before us, bordered by mountains to the east and west. At the back end of one clearing sat an ancient log cabin and small barn with a half mile of creek running a hundred yards below.

We drove the girls there the next day, unsure if they'd buy into our little fantasy. They piled out of the car and explored every nook and cranny of the cabin and barn before running back to us. "Can we have a horse?" Sally asked.

"See that black guy in the meadow?" their dad answered. "That's Prince—he goes with the place." That did it. They wanted to move the next day.

Unfortunately, it took nearly two years to get established at Wolf Lodge. Herb built his shop that fall before bad weather set in because he needed the space badly to store his equipment and to work. The winter passed quietly and quickly as we planned summer projects. I found in March that I was pregnant again at thirty-eight years old. Herb was fifty five.

When the snow melted that spring, Herb began building bunk beds into the cabin and cleaning out the barn. Moving to Wolf Lodge for the summer, we camped in the cabin and started projects, buying a few head of registered, polled Herefords and another horse for the girls. Herb found us an old Farmall tractor and built a trailer to carry the irrigation pipe we would use to draw water from the creek for raising hay, improving grazing, and watering the yard.

Announcing
NEW ULTRA-MODERN MODEL
that rolled off production line at
11:53 P. M. September 22, 1952,
at the Buroker Assembly Plant.

SPECIFICATIONS
SINGLE JET—Constructed with lots of metal,
360-degree circular
tail pipe, stick control, ball bearings throughout.
Empty weight, 7 lbs. 10.5 oz.

COLOR—Pink with faint blue lines

PERFORMANCE—A military secret.
However, it has broken through the sound barrier.

NAME—Herbert Cal Buroker (Kelly)
Can be seen at Buroker Hangar,
1522 N. Fourth St., Coeur d'Alene, Idaho.

Shortly after we moved back to Fourth Street that fall, our son Kelly was born September 22, 1952. A boy! The girls and I pampered our new family member that winter while Herb spent most every day at the ranch, feeding the cattle and repairing or rebuilding airplanes and boats.

The following spring he started building our ranch-style house and by June had laid the foundation and part of the cinder blocks. To save money he bought rough lumber, planing it into baseboards, window and door trim. While Herb built, I tackled the landscaping, leveling the huge expanse between the house and the creek with our tractor. The next step took some time. The kids and I raked out the large rocks, smoothed the dirt and planted grass. With the sprinklers going non-stop, I tackled the next item on my agenda. I hadn't gardened much since Olympia and couldn't wait to dig in the dirt. I put in fruit trees, raspberries, and a large vegetable plot. Every night my family looked like a washing machine's worst nightmare, but we were healthy and happy.

We finally made the plunge, selling the house in Coeur d'Alene and beginning the best two years of my life (the two years it took to get a telephone). As if by magic my migraines disappeared. I became a housewife and farmer while Herb continued his repair business. One fairly flat area behind our house stretched long enough for a small airplane to take-off or land if one knew the terrain well. When Herb completed a job (airplanes Herb repaired were dismantled and hauled in), I would fly it off our field when wind conditions permitted and deliver it to the owner at the Coeur d'Alene Air Terminal. We didn't talk about our field much since only experienced pilots could land and take off safely.

I soon found Herb liked animals but didn't want anything to do with farming; he'd much rather work in the shop. Not minding a bit, I plowed the garden plot and meadows and planted the crops. During harvest, I cut, raked and baled hay with Herb feeding the livestock only if the weather turned bad; otherwise, Kelly and I did it all.

From the time the baby was six months old, I took him everywhere with me. Having missed the joy of watching my girls grow during the war years, I made up my mind to relish every minute with Kelly, holding him in my arms even when I drove the tractor. If he fell asleep, I found a soft, grassy spot and laid him down until he woke.

As Kelly grew, I kept an eagle eye on him. The girls were big enough to take care of themselves, but Kelly was little and the creek dangerous. Friends, relatives, even strangers constantly warned me I'd never raise him that close to water. Consequently, I seldom let Kelly out of my sight. Since we lived a quiet life during these first years at the farm, Kelly didn't play much with kids other than his sisters. One day Herb and I were sitting on the patio after lunch, watching our three-year-old load his Tonka truck with rocks in the nearby dirt. Taffy, our Cocker Spaniel, sidled up to Kelly, sniffing his face and wagging her tail furiously. "Get away from me you yellow son-of-a-bitch," Kelly shouted. Speechless, I looked at Herb who I'd never heard swear.

"Where could he have heard that?" I asked.

Herb gave me a sheepish grin. "Yesterday, when I was under the car putting on the oil pan, I had both hands where I couldn't let go. Taffy licked my face, and I couldn't think of anything else to say."

Kelly developed a soft spot for all animals (even Taffy), nursing every stray that came around. One day we were working in the barn when I noticed a mouse trapped in the grain bin. "Go get the cat," I told him, knowing she'd be happy to dispose of the intruder. That afternoon I glanced in to see if she had done the job and found the mouse had escaped up a ladder of baling twine Kelly provided for the lucky rodent.

Like a lot of imaginative children, Kelly constantly told stories like the one about how he saw a tiger up on the ridge. We got so we didn't pay much attention. He came home one day after exploring the mountain east of the house with the Matthews kids whose family rented our old mill site a quarter mile up the creek.

"We found a cave full of dynamite, Mom!"

"Really!" I answered. "Bet that was fun."

"Yeah. It was."

I didn't think anything of it. Had there been a cave, I would have found it after walking every foot of our property several times looking for the milk cow and dead trees to cut for firewood.

A week later Kelly wanted to play with the Matthew kids again.

"Be back by noon." I said.

"Okay," he yelled as he slammed the screen door. It wasn't quite twelve, when an explosion rocked the ground. My knees went weak, but I forced myself to run to the tractor, my fingers fumbling with the starter, my foot flooring the accelerator. Herb sprinted from his shop to jump on behind. Unable to speak, we white-knuckled it to the Matthews.

When we got there, the kids ran out.

"Did ya hear the dynamite? Did ya?"

I still couldn't speak—just grabbed Kelly and bear hugged him.

Kelly Sidebar

One day the neighbor kids and I (five or six of us) found a case of dynamite somebody left after putting in a power or pipeline. The box had rotted away, and moss grew over the rubble. Unable to believe our luck, we picked up some of the dynamite and stacked it in a pile, carefully counting out 20 sticks. Apparently glycerine in the sticks we handled had seeped into the ground; we didn't dig deep enough to expose the live ones.

We took two sticks back to the Matthews' house (the parents were gone), lighted them with a match, then tossed them like firecrackers. In the process we actually cut one in half and tried to light the insides. Nothing happened.

When I got home, I told Mom and Dad we found dynamite in a cave (I stretched that part a little), so of course they figured I made up the story. A few days later Mr. Matthews found the dynamite and immediately headed to town for a cap and fuse. When he got home, we were playing about a hundred yards from the house. "Take cover he yelled." I wrapped my arms around a tree, and the next thing I knew I hit ground while fire, smoke and debris flew above the treetops followed by a huge column of smoke.

Of course we kids thought that was wild, neat stuff, exactly what we'd hoped for. In the house the impact had knocked all the pictures off the walls, the dishes out of the cupboards and broken several windows; what a mess! The next thing I remember was Mom and Dad rounding the corner on the tractor, its speeding wheels shaking so badly I thought they'd fall off. Mom looked as white as any white you'd ever seen. I'm sure she figured she'd be picking up body parts.

Jim Matthews stepped out the door a second later. He had investigated the kids' story, he told us, and had indeed found dynamite so decided to blast it to keep the them from getting hurt. We all took a deep breath and laughed. But that was the last of any brown hair on my head.

Though Kelly was the youngest, he certainly wasn't the only one to get into trouble. Each year I fenced my garden to protect it from cattle and deer. The peaceful sound of children yelling and laughing floated into the kitchen one afternoon as I fixed supper when suddenly I heard an awful scream. I ran out the door to find the kids peering over the garden fence at Sally who had climbed on the fence and jumped inside. Still screaming she stood on a board with one and a half inches of nail extending up through her shoe. Quickly opening the gate, I put my feet on either side of her foot to secure the board, took hold of her leg close to the ankle, and jerked up. Thankfully, as I unlaced her shoe, she quit screaming, but she still sobbed pitifully. I removed her shoe, yanked down the sock but couldn't find a scratch. The nail slid right between her toes.

Linda ran into a few scrapes too. Frequently during the summer months, young family members spent time with us on the creek. Our nephew, Dick Horch, had come to spend a week with us. One day we had just finished lunch, and Dick and Linda, both eight, had headed for the outdoors. Herb and I still talked at the table when Dick burst into the house, yelling, "Auntie Gladys!"

We always treated visiting children like our own, so I stopped him right there: "Wait until Uncle Herb and I finish talking." He said nothing more but hopped around like he needed to use the bathroom. After two or three minutes I finally said, "Dick, what was it you wanted?"

"Linda ran off the road on her bike on the high spot and went into the creek." We hit the door running. She could have been hurt, possibly drowned. (Does a mother ever know what to do or say in all circumstances?) We found Linda a few minutes later scratched, bruised, but struggling to push her bike, which she certainly didn't plan to leave, up the embankment.

The creek Linda fell in seemed to gather kids by the dozens since the area's best swimming hole sat right under our bridge. Ducks liked it too, wild mallards flying in almost every evening and staying till morning. We noticed one day something was killing them—more than likely weasels. Herb decided to tame the ducks enough to coax them into the barn at night. That evening he put out chicken feed in a line from the creek to the barn. It took several tries to coax the birds up to the buildings, but the next night when he opened the barn door, they all waddled right in. Herb shut the door and let them out first thing the next morning. They came back every evening after that for their handout. I have no idea what Herb paid out for chicken feed the twenty years we lived at Wolf Lodge, but the enjoyment he got was worth it.

Domesticating wildlife just seemed natural on the farm. We took another stab at it one July morning when Linda came running into the shop to tell Herb a logging truck had killed a doe near our house. Because of the season, we figured she probably had a fawn. After a quick search, we found the baby, probably two weeks old, in a grassy, sheltered spot near the road. We carried him to the barn and fed him with a lamb's bottle. After a week to let him adjust, Herb opened the barn door to free him, but he always came back when he was hungry. Our little friend quickly became the neighborhood pet, roaming the valley and begging

158

grain off everyone. He'd even follow Kelly on his bicycle like a dog and return home when Kelly turned back.

The yearling survived the first hunting season and winter, but we worried about his safety that next fall. To discourage anyone from shooting him, we tied red ribbons to his antlers. On opening day of hunting season, a neighbor up the road calmly pulled a rifle out of his truck and shot our friend as he grazed in the man's back yard. Everyone in the valley felt sick. To me, he might as well have shot the family dog.

Besides water fowl and deer, we occasionally saw bear, especially in the fall when they raided the apple orchard. One day Dove Kuczinski, our neighbor to the north, suggested we pick huckleberries at our favorite spot near Skitwish Ridge. Dove

Tame deer that roamed Wolf Lodge Valley.

and I separated, planning to meet back at the truck for lunch. I climbed an embankment through thick brush, finding berries as big as the tip of my finger. The morning passed pleasantly until I heard the brush cracking. "That you, Dove?" I hollered, thinking she was close by. She didn't answer, so I stood up. A huge black bear sat eating huckleberries about 30 feet to my right. It looked at me, stuffed another paw full of berries in its mouth, then moseyed up the hill, never giving me another glance.

That's how our life went those first five years, my family and I celebrating the coming and going of the seasons without the stress or frantic activity associated with war and running a business. Even so, disaster of sorts did visit us in a much different way. Ted Miles, who lived on Blue Creek just the other side of Meyers Hill, called us one day late May 1957. "Is Wolf Lodge Creek high?" he asked.

"Just like it's been the last couple of weeks," Herb answered. "Bout normal for spring run-off."

"Blue Creek's higher than usual," Ted said. "Seems to be coming up fast today." We had heavy rain for the past few days but didn't think much about Ted's call since spring runoff was about over.

I'll never forget the shock the next morning. Herb crawled out of bed first, like he always did. When he flipped the light switch in the bathroom, nothing happened. "Hmm-m-m," he thought. "Better check the wiring." When he tried to start the coffee a few minutes later, he discovered we had no power. Then he glanced out the picture window.

Alders floated past his line of vision like images on a movie screen. The out-of-control creek had not only ripped loose the bridge and dumped it who-knows-where but surrounded our house and barn like islands in a lake. "Gladys," he roared. "Get up!"

"Where do you suppose the cows and calves are?" I asked once I could speak again.

"I'll check on 'em," Herb said.

Putting on his hip boots, Herb struggled across the short distance to the barn and found Prince and the cows huddled on a high spot close to the building. He saddled Prince and rode south along a high mountain trail to the Rider ranch where he discovered the road to U. S. Highway 90 intact. At least we could get out if conditions worsened. Herb returned, packed clothes for Sally and Linda, and took them on horseback to the Riders, so they could finish their last week of school. Once he safely deposited the girls, Herb set out in search of eight missing calves. He found them about a half mile from the barn, bunched together on a little island still above water. Loading each frantic little critter on the horse, he carried it back to the barn.

We sat down to discuss our next move. Herb and I both worried about Kelly's safety around so much water. Although he put up one heck of a battle, we sent him back to Spokane with my sister who had driven out to see if we were okay. The next three weeks challenged our resources. We used the fireplace to keep warm and cooked outside on an improvised stove made of concrete blocks topped with a metal rack. We caught rainwater to drink and used creek water for washing and doing dishes.

When the water finally receded, Washington Water Power reset the downed power poles and made other repairs. Meanwhile Herb saddled Prince and searched for our bridge, finding it jammed against some trees on the south end of our property.

We lost our bridge during Wolf Lodge Creek flood - May 1957.

Surprisingly, the bridge appeared intact, and the pilings from which it was ripped were still in place in front of our house. Greatly relieved not to have to build a new bridge, we now faced how to get the bridge back to the creek. Herb rented a large caterpillar tractor, hauled the bridge back, and reanchored it to the pilings.

Although it took a couple of months to dry out, we had our farm back to normal before long. By now the girls wanted to join 4-H with their friends, and before we knew it Herb and I were knee-high in projects. It didn't take much arm-twisting from participating parents before I found myself leader of the Harmony Hustlers 4-H Club for the next fifteen years; Herb was the leader the five years following that. The club included kids from ten to eighteen from Wolf Lodge, Blue Creek, and Sunnyside to whom I taught entomology, forestry, weeds and junior leadership. Herb taught tractor maintenance and woodworking. Over the fifteen years, our members won many honors, including state and national awards. In 1962 I was honored as Outstanding 4-H Leader of the Year by the Cooperative Extension Service, U.S. Department of Agriculture and the University of Idaho.

When I wasn't outdoors farming or working with kids, I took every chance I had to hunt and fish. The Spurbecks, neighbors who lived on the creek, hunted with Herb and I, usually for several days at a time, and occasionally Anne and I would day hunt too. "You should see the elk sign up on Spade Mountain!" Anne told me excitedly one evening. "Let's go hunting first thing in the morning."

"I can't, Anne. Too much work to do."

"The work'll keep. Hunting season's almost over!" We left before daylight in Anne's Jeep, hitting Spade Mountain by first dawn. Agreeing to meet at the Jeep at noon, I set out slowly, moving quietly a little ways, then stopping to look and listen. About an hour later I stood against an old fir, carefully scanning the tree line when I thought I heard the brush crack. I focused my eyes in the direction of the sound, every sense alert.

I heard rustling again—louder this time—then spotted a rack of antlers coming up the hill. I readied my .32 calibre carbine and waited, afraid to even breathe. The elk, looking about the size of an elephant, didn't seem in any hurry, taking a couple of steps, then stopping to look around. "What if he smells me," I thought. "I'd better shoot."

I carefully aimed and pulled the trigger. CLICK. Darn! I'd forgotten the safety. The elk lifted his head in my direction. Trying to be calm, I pushed the safety to "off" and shot again. He turned and crashed down the hill. Just sick, I wondered how I could have missed at that range. I followed his trail, thinking I might get another shot. About a hundred yards into a thick growth of buck brush and huckleberries, I found him down and dead, the bullet having entered the neck just behind the head.

All I had with me was an old hunting knife. With some effort I pulled the elk's head back and cut the throat to bleed him while I waited for Anne with her good knife and saw—she <u>must</u> have heard the shot. After a few impatient moments, I started to dress-out the carcass. It felt like cutting leather with a table knife. I know it took me an hour or more to gut him.

While I worked, I heard a car on the road down the hill and decided maybe Anne couldn't find me. Once the elk was ready to haul out, I decided to head back to our rig. I marked the trail down the mountainside and, laid a small log against the roadside to remember where to park. By the time I rounded the last corner and found the Jeep, I felt exhausted, my adrenaline rush just about depleted. Anne sat on the running board, her head in her hands. When she spotted me, she started to cry.

"What's wrong Anne?" I asked.

"I heard the shot and tried to find you," she sobbed, hugging me tightly. "I called and called but you didn't answer."

Once she calmed down, I told Anne I'd bagged an elk. She even smiled at that. We parked the jeep next to the five-foot-high bank where I marked the trail and headed up to complete the job. After quartering the carcass, we wound baling twine around each quarter, then looped it over our shoulders down to our waists and dragged the load to the jeep. I figured with a little luck we could back the pickup into the bank and load it without help.

Only a hunter would understand how many times we fell with the elk quarter landing on top of us. Each time we took a spill, we'd laugh hysterically until we had enough energy to go on. By the time the last quarter was down, Anne said, "Let's leave the head and rack."

"No!" I answered. "I'll get it myself." We practically crawled up that hill for the last load. Back at the road, I backed the jeep to the bank. While Anne pushed the quarters, I pulled them into the jeep bed. Driving home we should have been exhausted, but we were so excited we didn't feel it.

When we got to our place, Herb couldn't believe his eyes. He kept saying, "How did you girls do it?" And when I showed

Gladys and Anne Spurbeck after successful hunt on Spade Mt. - 1968.

him the knife I used to dress the elk, he just shook his head. The October 14, 1964, *Coeur d'Alene Press* ran a picture of Anne and me with our trophy head in the back of the Jeep. The caption read,

WHAT WEAKER SEX?—These two women pulled off what many male hunters would never attempt after one of them shot an 800-pound bull elk in the Spade mountain area of Coeur d'Alene National Forest. Mrs. Herb Buroker, who shot the animal with her .32 calibre carbine, and Mrs. Anne Spurbeck, dressed it, and with the aide of some bailing twine rolled and dragged it down 1,000 feet of mountainside, piled it into the back of their jeep and headed for home. There they were greeted by Mrs. Buroker's husband who made no attempt to conceal his amazement when the women unloaded their prize.

Chapter 14: The Kids' Perspective

Our years at Wolf Lodge were perhaps the most formative in the kids' childhoods. Their combined perspectives about our lives help us understand who we are today.

LINDA

"I was really confused about Mom. The classic "mother" of the Fifties was Donna Reed. She was supposed to float to the door in a shirtwaist dress to welcome the kids and their friends. She was supposed to have spent the day baking cookies. Beaver Cleaver's mother was like that. Harriet Nelson was like that. They never did anything but take care of the family which they were thrilled to do.

Mom was different. When I wanted to bring friends home, I worried sometimes, wondering, "What are they going to think when they see Mom in a pair of jeans, driving a tractor or something?" Once I got over that, we had lots of fun cause Mom never let us down. She took us on hay rides, fixed picnic lunches, and became one of the most active 4-H leaders in the state.

"Do you really wish that you would have been a boy?" I would ask Mom now and then. I couldn't figure out how she could be such a good mother, enjoy having children, yet wear pants, short hair, and work like a man. In fact it caused me a lot of problems in my young womanhood. People told me from the time I was little that I looked and acted like a miniature Mom— even down to the short haircut she insisted on. Knowing I didn't want to be boyish—like Mom—I overdid being feminine, growing my hair long when I left home just to prove it. (Only in my forties have I realized short hair can be wonderful.)

Though Mom was more than gracious when my friends came over, she needed the solitude of the farm—she's sort of singular that way. She didn't want to fly an airplane or see any of the airport crowd. When we first moved, dozens of people seemed to drop by, expecting to be entertained, but eventually the drop-ins dwindled and then pretty much disappeared. It was like Mom temporarily put flying in the closet and shut the door. Both Sally and I felt a little sorry for Dad and remember him sneaking to town to hang around his pals.

Mom's behavior never seemed to bother Dad much. He adored her and would do anything she wanted. They were friends and partners, working well together on building the house and running the farm. But in the parenting department, Mom was definitely in charge—especially with us kids—while Dad remained more detached. Mom has this amazing ability to let people know exactly what she wants them to do without saying much.

On the rare occasion when that didn't work, she spanked us, more often me since I challenged her a lot. People would remark, "You have your mother's Irish temper." Where Sally would do exactly what Mom asked, I would yell, "Why CAN'T I do that?" Dad even slapped me one time for being rude to Mom.

Dad was fun loving and silly, but in many ways he kept his distance. I was astounded when Mom told me he spent hours with me when I had polio, massaging my legs every day. Had it not been for his constant care, I may have never recovered. But most of my life I missed his participation, the closeness I needed. Sure, he came to games and school activities, was supportive, but seldom intimate. I missed that a lot.

Mom was always there when we needed her. When I tell friends now that she embarrassed me, they can't believe I would have been anything but thrilled to have a mother like her. I agree wholeheartedly now I'm old enough to understand. The sense of calm she now possesses seems to have developed the last few years. I think she had quite a temper as a young person (that's why she and her father clashed so badly), but that temperament gives her the spark that makes her bigger-than-life—so full of the devil. I love her more and accept myself more, knowing these traits make great things possible.

SALLY

Dad was a romantic, a lover of life, and a consummate trickster. I can still remember one prank he pulled that embarrassed me to death. He had a funny friend named Alex who also flew— well, sort of. Alex wouldn't fly to towns without railroad tracks because he couldn't read aerial maps. One day Dad and Alex went fishing and later took me to the airport. On the way back, we decided to stop for dinner, and Dad grabbed his fishing basket on the way in. When the waitress took our order, he casually pulled out a trout and asked the waitress to fry it up. I remember how everyone laughed, and then the waitress actually did it!

Dad scared me as a child because he loved pranks and I was afraid he might pull one if I flew with him. As an adult I had more trust and understanding. One day we had two J-3's and one J-5 at Cavanaugh's Bay. Dad wanted to take off in formation. I remember my elation as the two of us accelerated side by side, bouncing all over the grass runway. Dad just loved it. "That's what flying used to be," he told me.

Though he longed for the "old" days, I know he and Mom jointly decided to move to the farm. He loved country life and animals. (Though he could butcher rabbits and chickens, he couldn't face killing the cows over which he pampered and fussed.) He wanted to move, still it must have felt uncomfortable being unemployed. That's hard on a person, to work ten hours a day for years and have a real purpose each morning, then to try unsuccessfully to make a living at farming. He started taking odd jobs, repairing boats and aircraft. Dad was terribly conscientious and proud of his work. What I admired most was his love for helping people. Farmers up and down the valley knew Dad would trade welding and mechanical work at no charge: "I'll fix your combine if you'll help us get in the hay."

With Dad in the shop most of the time, Mother provided well for us–so well, in fact, he didn't need to give much input. When I needed a new dress for a special occasion, she always had a secret stash which she'd give to me saying, "Don't tell Dad."

Even though he remained somewhat in the background, I felt Dad equally able to care for us. Heck, he even taught me how to make milk gravy, and some of my favorite recipes like head cheese and applesauce come from Dad's family.

Though he seemed remote sometimes, Dad was there when I needed him the most. After I married, I had a frustrating weekend with my husband, who wanted to go to the car races while I yearned to shop in Spokane. I knew Dad had been good to mother and knew how to make a marriage work. When I told him my problem, he thought it over and then said, "Over the years your mother planned things I didn't want to do, but I'd go along anyway. I never had a bad time, and sometimes I even had fun." That helped me a lot. At first glance Dad didn't seem to take life seriously, but I think he really had a handle on things.

As an adult I've had trouble making decisions. Mom guided me so deftly as a child, I developed little confidence in myself, feeling timid and too much of a girl, in the face of my parents' fortitude. "Should I have been a boy?" I asked myself many times. Mom never said or did anything to make me feel that way, and Dad spoiled me rotten. My fondest childhood memory is the Sunday mornings that Dad took me with him to the drugstore. He would buy a Sunday paper and I was guaranteed a new comic book, crayons, or an ice cream cone.

KELLY

The only disagreement I ever saw between Mom and Dad seems comical in retrospect. While we built our second house at Wolf Lodge, the family camped in Dad's shop which had no plumbing. It was the first day of fishing season when Mom noticed someone down in the creek.

"Herb, tell that man to leave," she demanded. "I'm not going to the outhouse until he's gone."

"Tell him yourself," Dad replied, busy with something.

The more Mom insisted, the more Dad refused. I don't know how Mom resolved her immediate problem, but I do know they didn't speak that day. Maybe they felt safe getting angry about something so silly. Serious problems they always talked out in mild-mannered discussions, never yelling, never getting upset, always coming to mutual agreements.

Because of the age difference between Dad and me, I discussed more personal problems with Mom, things I didn't understand.

"Why do I get pimples?" I asked her one day.

"Well let's sit down and talk about it," she said. She must have noticed my body changing and picked that opportunity to explain the facts of life. I don't remember talking like that with Dad. Instead, he and I would discuss building projects in the shop and working on my bike or car, teaching me everything with the patience of a saint.

Though I spent lots of time with Dad, the things I did with Mom stand out in my memories—activities most moms would never consider. Besides carting me along for chores, she often met me at the school bus with our motorcycle and my 410 shot gun. Off we'd go grouse hunting on the logging roads, taking turns driving while the other one shot. It's unbelievable the fun we had and the number of grouse we brought home.

Mom also taught me to fly. Even at 16, it didn't take me long to realize I liked flying but not piloting. When I backpeddled about learning, neither Mom nor Dad ever pressured me. I felt differently about sky diving, though, in love with danger, with the thrill of free-falling toward the earth. About the time I learned, Mom started flying the hot air balloon. Skydivers always wanted to show in their log book they would jump from anything—the more unorthodox, the better. A day or two before my birthday, I had just finished a jump when Mom walked over and said, "We've got about an hour's worth of light left. Pack your chute, and I'll let you jump from the balloon."

Man, was I excited. Climbing in for my first balloon ride ever, I had no idea what the next few moments would bring. Mom gave the balloon as much heat as she could since the sun was going down. "If you're going to jump, better go now," she said after about five minutes

When I started getting out, I realized I'd never parachuted from something so slow-moving. When you jump from an airplane, 80 miles of air speed help control the body's position relative to the ground. You don't want to get upside down as the chute could wrap around your arm or leg and malfunction. A bit nervous, I finally climbed out and hung on the basket's edge. I'll tell you, that was a feat in itself. Screwing up my courage, I let go and tumbled like a leaf, flipping and flopping, losing altitude fast, trying desperately to get face down. I finally opened the chute far below the 2000 foot legal limit. Looking back it seems stupid, but my instructors drilled into my head to be in position before pulling the cord. I think I scared Mom pretty badly that day.

Mom's version—sidebar

Kelly had taken up sky diving and had made about 30 jumps when he asked me to take him up so he could jump from the balloon. I didn't want him to do it and kept putting him off. It could be done, I knew, as I remembered seeing a balloon jump while on my motorcycle trip in 1936. Risky as it was, I had a hard time putting off Kelly who knew the risks I had taken parachuting as a youngster. I finally gave in.

It was just before sunset, so time was important. Kelly said he thought 3,000 feet would be enough altitude, but he'd like more if there was time. When we got to 3,000, he climbed out facing the basket with his toes clinging to the narrow ledge at the bottom. I know he wanted more altitude, so I continued to climb but was anxious as it was getting dark, and I was drifting west toward Mt. Spokane. When he jumped, I watched him drop as I gained another 2,000 feet of altitude. "Why doesn't he open his chute?" I thought as he fell and fell and fell, my heart in my throat. I knew he needed momentum, but he was almost to the ground. It finally

opened, and he landed about 30 seconds later.

Taking a deep breath to calm myself, I began looking for a place to land and spotted a field near Round Mountain. By now it was so dark I could have easily flown into a fence or power line. Though no roads cut near the field, I needed to get down-immediately. If Sally couldn't find me, I figured I could spend the night wrapped in the envelope to keep warm. The air was so calm I set down easily and deflated the envelope, preparing it for packing. Suddenly Sally, who had found an abandoned logging road to the field, spoke to me— I hadn't heard her coming and jumped about two feet. By separating the basket and envelope, we lifted them into the pickup and headed home. Kelly was happy and did not ask to jump again, thank goodness, though I think everyone else with a parachute did.

I think Dad liked to hunt and fish just about as much as Mom. Every year on the first day of fishing season Dad would wake me at 4:30 a.m. Still in a fog, I'd bounce off the walls, trying to get on my shoes and clothes. We'd head to the bridge across the creek right below the house to the deep hole where I had already spotted (and named) the biggest fish. I'd do my best to hook him, and then we'd tramp up and down the rest of the creek. I'm sure Dad tired of this since I fished year round anyway, but he made me feel like the most important kid in the world.

When I grew big enough to carry a gun, Dad taught me how to hunt. The first deer I ever shot at I got "buck fever" and missed. Dad didn't laugh; he just never let me live it down. Another instance ended up a lot more embarrassing. One of the neighbors told us he had spotted a sow bear with her cubs up on the ridge.

"Let's go up the hill and see if we can find it," Dad said.

"There's not a chance in hell we'll find that bear," I thought to myself, but I grabbed Mom's 32 special Weber action hunting rifle and walked behind Dad up the mountain.

"Go ahead n' walk down the trail. I'll be right behind," Dad told me after a bit. Not much later, the bushes rustled off to my left, and my jaw dropped when that sow walked right in front of me. When the lever is thrown open, the Weber will pick up a shell if there's not one already in the chamber. If there is, it will eject the existing cartridge before picking up a new shell. My hands shaking, I threw the lever open and ejected a shell.

"That can't be right," I thought nervously, so I closed it, flipped it, and another shell flew out. I emptied all the shells while the bear stood and watched. Finally realizing my mistake, I shot, but by then the sow'd taken off running. Dad collapsed on the ground laughing, while red-faced and furious, I demanded why he hadn't shot. I'll tell you I was one upset little kid, but I eventually learned to think before jumping into things.

Dad, who loved a good laugh, believed a practical joke the height of entertainment. One year at a Buroker family reunion in Walla Walla, Dad put on a grey beard and a shaggy, grey wig streaked with black. Then he donned big wide sunglasses, some old grey pants rolled up at the cuff, and an old striped T-shirt with "I am a Jack that looks like a Jill and smells like a John" printed on the back. He wandered around the park like a bum, making rude comments to his family (who hoped he'd go away) until he finally broke up laughing and revealed his identity. Everyone loved being around Dad.

In spite of his silly side, Dad was considerate, knowing kids need choices too. Every year on our annual fishing trip to the coast, he would do something I've never forgotten. I just loved hamburgers and still do. Taking me aside before we headed out, he'd tell me, "Now Kelly, any time you want a hamburger, you can have one. It doesn't have to be when we stop for lunch. Any time you want one, if there's a place, we'll get it." I know what a pain that must have been, trying to find a burger stand whenever I got an urge.

Though he was a nice guy, Dad wasn't afraid to stand up for his principles. "If you really believe in something," he told me one day, " I'll back you 100%." I knew from that moment I'd get his support when I needed it. The courage Dad taught me came naturally to him. One day a guy fishing in front of the house refused to go when Mom spoke to him.

"I'm not leaving," he told her, getting more belligerent the second time she asked. Dad, still wearing his tool belt, walked down to confront the trespasser. I knew the guy would never catch fish cause I was throwing rocks in the creek, so I guess it was his attitude that got Dad riled.

"If you want me out, you're gonna have to come get me. Better bring your hammer," he sneered. Dad unhooked his tool belt.

"I don't need a hammer," he answered, walking right into the creek. The guy bolted across the creek to his car with his tail between his legs. I thought that was great—Dad was quite a man!

Chapter 15: Who'd Have Ever Thought I'd Be a Nurse!

"What's this?" Herb roared one morning as he opened the mail. "Our property taxes are $400. That's highway robbery!" Seldom seeing Herb so upset, I knew we were in for some changes.

Since the girls were gone by 1965 and Kelly was nearly finished with school, we decided to sell the farm at Wolf Lodge and build a new home. Herb found 120 acres on Fernan Hill close to Coeur d'Alene where we started by drilling a well. These plans came to a halt, though, when our farm's buyer convinced Herb to buy back five acres on the north end of the Wolf Lodge property and build there instead. I guess he thought Herb would make a great neighbor.

We moved into our new house—split level with a daylight basement—the fall of 1966. By spring I had itchy feet. After a brief stint at job hunting, I found a job taking bets for the horse races at Kootenai County Fair Grounds. My neighbor, Jean Holt, got a kick hearing my stories about work. A plain, raw-boned woman, Jean seemed stern on the surface but she had a terrific sense of humor underneath—just my kind of gal. Since the track constantly needed help, I suggested she ride to town with me and apply. My boss put her to work the next day. "Pulled one over on him," she said with the tiniest of smiles as we left his office.

We loved the excitement of the track that summer, and I wondered what I'd do once the season ended. One August morning I noticed in the *Coeur d'Alene Press* that North Idaho College planned to offer a practical nursing program sponsored by Kootenai Memorial Hospital, Pinewood Manor, and the State Board of Education. Excited, I picked up the phone and called Jean. "Are you interested?" I asked.

"Well, I guess so," she said.

The next day we met with Clarence Haught, NIC's director

of vocational education. He patiently explained the program but told us we were too late. The application deadline was two days away. "Sorry ladies," he said, "but it's impossible to get three letters of recommendation and your high school transcripts in time."

As we left the college, I told Jean, "How does he know what we can't do in two days?" Stopping at the nearest restaurant, we ordered coffee and plotted our strategy. We figured the recommendations would be no problem and listed the names of people we needed to call. The transcripts, however, would be tougher. The minute we got home we contacted our high schools. They promised to mail transcripts to the college that day.

Two days later we visited Mr. Haught again, handing him the recommendations. "Didn't think it could be done," he said with a laugh. "I sure was surprised when I got your transcripts this morning!" He told us our applications would be considered along with the others. "We'll take only ten students this first class." Deflated, we walked to the car. How could we compete with all those bright, young girls?

I don't remember how many days passed. It seemed like a hundred. Finally the employment office called one morning. "Are you still interested in working for Pendar?" a man's voice asked. Earlier that year I had applied at the electronics firm in Post Falls. Now they finally had an opening.

"Yes," I told him. That was that.

Disappointed, I cried on Herb's shoulder at lunch. "Why don't you put Pendar off a few more days," he suggested. "NIC still might call." Not five minutes after he walked out the door, the phone rang again. "Congratulations, Mrs. Buroker," Mr. Haught's secretary said. "You've been selected for the nursing program." I hung up elated. "Should I call Jean?" I asked myself. "What if she didn't get in." Just then Jean phoned. She too had been accepted.

During our first eight weeks as students, we studied theory and observed nurses at Sunset Terrace Nursing Home. Diane

Granger, RN, was our instructor. Although I didn't earn A's this first leg of our journey, I held my own. At the end of eight weeks, Diane capped us at a special ceremony at North Idaho College. Next, we started clinical and the most terrifying learning experience of my life. In addition to taking three hours of theory in the conference room at Kootenai Memorial Hospital, we were to work five hours each day in nursery, obstetrics, geriatrics, pediatrics, surgical or medical, along with emergency room and central service training.

Clinical didn't seem to be a problem. But after thirty-six years out of school, I just couldn't get the hang of anatomy and physiology. No matter how hard I worked, I couldn't pronounce or spell the names of muscle groups, much less locate them in the body. Quite frankly, I was in bad shape. Finally I told Jean I planned to quit. Word must have spread quickly because everyone in the class made it her business to talk to me. I agreed to stick it out thirty more days. By then something clicked, and I figured out how to study.

We were all novices but none more so than our teacher Diane. (She was Diane now, not Mrs. Granger). It was bad enough that we were her first class ever but worse that over half of us were older than she. Eager to learn and full of questions, I decided after a few futile attempts to back off. Rather than risk a wrong answer, Diane would simply tell me to look it up.

In a sense we were all guinea pigs that year. Diane had never taught, and we had never been near hospitals. What a setup for fun! At our first session in clinical, Diane gave us our assignments for the next day. She sent Jackie Anderson, just out of high school, to X-ray where she was told they would do G.I.'s. Jackie was thrilled. To her, G.I.'s meant guys. The next day, Jackie sat five hours watching clinicians X-ray patients' gastrointestinal systems (not a young man in the bunch). The rest of us got a good laugh.

Diane took us into the treatment room on Medical East a few days later to demonstrate how to drape a patient. When modeling such procedures, Diane used a life-sized manikin the hospital staff had dubbed, "Mary Chase." Placing the manikin on a treatment table, Diane had just started when she got a phone call. The minute she left, the mischief began. Jean grabbed Mary and stood her in a corner behind the group. Then Fay Lee climbed onto the treatment table, and we covered her with a drape.

Much to our surprise, Diane returned with a visitor. "You all know Mr. Haught," Diane said. "He dropped by to visit our class." We glanced nervously at one another, but it was too late to stop now.

"Mr. Haught," Diane said, doing her best rendition of a teacher. "Our clinical experience today is how to properly drape a patient for an exam." She then turned to the table and said, "You should never cover a patient's head" at which she pulled back the drape.

"Boo!" Fay yelled. Diane jumped a least three feet, turning crimson from head to toe while Mr. Haught laughed until tears ran down his face. From that point on it was tricks until graduation.

We pulled another one in the conference room during class one day after Diane had taught the lesson and told us to study the last hour of class. As soon as she was out of sight (we could see into the lobby through one-way windows), we put our books in our chairs and shoved the chairs against the table. Then we hid in the meditation room which joined the conference room and also had one-way windows. About 15 minutes later Diane walked back into the conference room, then exited, walking twice as fast toward the information desk.

The attendant shook her head vigorously in response to Diane's questions after which Diane headed quickly down the hall. As soon as she disappeared, we hurried back in, opened our books, and began studying like mad when she came back a few moments later with the Director of Nursing, Betty Anderson. We paid no attention to them until Diane started to laugh. You might say she had her hands full with this class.

Diane soon figured out that Jean and I were behind most of

the deviltry. But I certainly didn't come up with the plot to fake an error in the nursery—I knew that meant trouble. The class outvoted me, and plans began. Since Hilde Hartman was one of the class angels, we decided to organize the incident when she was assigned to the nursery. That way Diane would never suspect foul play. Grace Harmon, the charge nurse for OB and the nursery, agreed to go along if we cleared every detail with her. Next, we went to Pearl Isaacson, the new director of nursing, who also agreed to participate.

We chose a day when two baby girls were scheduled to be discharged, one in the morning and one at 2:00 p.m. After the first proud parents took home their baby, we gave both charts to the head nurse for safe keeping. Then the action began. "Mrs. Granger...Mrs. Granger," the pager boomed throughout the hospital. "Contact nursery immediately." When Diane called, Hilde started sobbing hysterically. "I don't know what to do," she blubbered. "I sent home the wrong baby."

I was sitting at the desk in OB updating

Gladys, Herb and granddaughter, Anneliese, following graduation from North Idaho College LPN course.

my charts when Diane bustled by into the nursery. Fifteen minutes later she came back out and headed down the hall. Even from my ringside seat, I couldn't see that anything was bothering her. But from what Pearl later told us, Diane walked into her office, sat down, and started to cry. Feeling badly that our joke had been so upsetting, Pearl fessed up. This time we had gone too far.

We behaved ourselves only until graduation day. In celebration we jacked up Pearl and Diane's cars and put blocks under the rear axles. We also got Mr. Jepsen, the hospital administrator, by mounting a coyote head on his car's front grill. After we'd filled a couple of the doctor's cars with bed pans, we finally ran out of steam. Shortly after graduation Jean and I drove to Boise to take the State Board examinations for Licensed Practical Nurse. We both passed with flying colors.

Kootenai hired me as night nurse in OB-GYN, 11 pm to 7:30 am. On my first night, the off-shift nurse gave me a report for each patient on the floor (just as I had learned in clinical). After she left, I checked each person, recording vital signs and seeing to her comfort (just as I had been taught). Finished, I headed back to an empty nurse's station to update charts, expecting a supervisor to show up any time. When no one came, it dawned on me. My job—my life and death job—was to care for these people.

Now that Jean and I held both graduate status and jobs, we felt it our duty to initiate the next batch of nursing students. The first day of clinical, Diane took the group on a tour of the facility. While they wandered around in another part of the hospital, Jean and I snuck into the morgue. I pulled a gurney into the center of the room, and Jean climbed on. Covering her with a sheet, I went back to work. When the students walked in, Diane began telling them about procedure in the morgue. Jean groaned softly. Diane, by now a consummate actress, jumped and looked around. Then when she resumed talking, Jean moaned a little louder. Again Diane glanced nervously around the room before continuing her lecture. The third time this happened, one of the students backed up. "Someone's alive in here," she stammered, her face dead white. Jean threw back the sheet, and the whole bunch screamed and charged for the door. We felt we had gotten them off to a good start.

During the next few years, I found more satisfaction in nursing than in any job I've ever had. Even though I'd walk in the house exhausted at the end of a shift, I'd still feel great about my day. Getting along well with patients seemed to be my forte—even the difficult ones. One terminal cancer patient really sticks in my memory because no one could please the guy. I just did what he asked, talked to him, and listened—really listened. When he died, the family gave me gifts. I have never felt so needed or so gratified.

Four years of nursing was all my body could take. By 1970 I was 58, and lifting patients became too much. When Mr. Jepsen, the hospital administrator, offered me a position as Inservice Coordinator, I reluctantly accepted. From my basement office I organized new employee orientations and nursing inservices and also headed the hospital safety committee. Less than a year later Mr. Jepsen promoted me again to Director of Hospital Education and to a real office on the main floor complete with a secretary, Twyla Kemp. My new duties included providing inservices for all hospital personnel as well as developing an educational program for patients.

I'd just figured out that job when a very different responsibility came my way. Mr. Jepsen added central service to my duties and two more words to my title: Director of Education/ Central Service. All sterilization took place in Central Service, a semi sterile area adjoining surgery. Personnel working there scrubbed and changed in an entry room and wore hospital gowns, caps, and shoe covers. All supplies for CS came through the entrance room where staff wiped them clean before placing them on the shelves. I supervised thirteen CS employees working three shifts, seven days a week.

I guess I handled that one okay because in 1975 Jepsen offered me a position in purchasing. This meant giving up the Education Department but keeping CS. "I'm interested," I told him, "but I want to keep Twyla and need to know about salary."

"You're already making what the job allows, according to hospital policy," he told me, "so I'll change the title to Director of Materials which will allow you an increase." I took the job, and it wasn't long until Twyla joined me. I held this position until my retirement in 1980.

Chapter 16: The Best Friend I Ever Had

The hospital staff seemed, for all the world, like a close-knit family. Just five of us gals knew that Code 25 really meant, "Hit the Holiday at the end of shift." It just seemed natural that sooner or later Pearl Isaacson and I would become buddies. Not only had she been my clinical supervisor, but she had taken part in our best nursing school pranks. One day after I had been working at the hospital for some time, we sipped a cocktail at the Holiday. "Herb asked me to pick up some airplane parts after work tomorrow at Felts Field," I told her. "Would ya like to come along?"

"Yes!" she answered, her eyes bright. "I've never flown before."

I knew Pearl well enough to tell she could take a joke, so I planned to have some fun. Once off the ground, Pearl barraged me with questions about the instruments, straining her eyes to pick out landmarks and practically hyperventilating when we landed at Felts. We picked up Herb's order and lifted off in less than an hour. Giving Pearl ten minutes to settle down, I began my charade.

"Pearl, I don't know what's going on," I told her. "I've got a killer headache." Putting my head in my hands, I added, "Can you reach my purse in the back seat?" Pearl handed it over, and I faked swallowing some medication. "I'm feeling pretty bad," I managed a moment later. "You'll have to take the wheel."

I had the airplane trimmed, so it could fly by itself, but Pearl didn't know that. She grabbed the wheel and worked it over real good. "Do you think you can land it?" I mumbled a minute later.

Accustomed to handling emergencies in the hospital, she sat a little straighter and said, "Just tell me what to do." I know she would have tried, but I burst out laughing. Relaxing, she slugged my arm—hard-knowing she'd been had. After we calmed down a little, she said, "I saw a movie once where a woman landed an airplane after her husband had a heart attack. I figured if she could do it, I could too." I bet she could have.

This started an eleven year friendship with the best buddy I ever had. At 4'11" and ninety five pounds, Pearl was no bigger than a minute, but she could work circles around the rest of us. As Kootenai Memorial's director of nursing, she could be vivacious and friendly, yet tough as nails when necessary.

Unfortunately, Pearl was not destined for a bright future. Only months after she remarried the summer of '69 and a year after we made our first flight, Pearl's doctor diagnosed her with breast cancer. Finding tumors spread everywhere, the surgical team pronounced her terminal in spite of a mastectomy but recommended chemotherapy to slow down the process. Needless to say, chemo right after surgery sent Pearl into a physical and emotional tailspin. Visiting her hospital room one day after my shift, I found Pearl lifting weights with her right arm, trying to regain its strength. She looked small and sadly vulnerable, yet sweat beaded her determined face as she worked.

"I know!" I said after watching a moment. "I have an exercise for your arm

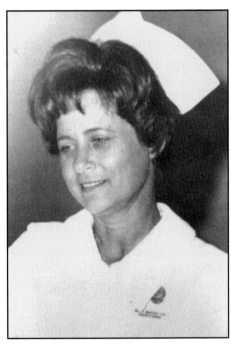

Pearl Mancheni, director of Nursing at Kootenai Memorial Hospital.

you'll love. Wanna learn to fly the Piper J3?"

"Really think it'd help?" she asked, brightening a little.

"Sure." I said, excited. "You'll have to use your right hand on the stick, and your left hand on the throttle. The back and forth motion will work just like weights, but it'll be lots more fun!"

As soon as she was able, we headed to the airport. I found Pearl an attentive and eager student. At first she used both hands when landing until she built up a little strength. Gradually she grew stronger, and it seemed like no time until she soloed. Thrilled, she said, "You're right. Flying is what I need. What a crazy thing to do at this stage of my life!"

Every week found us at the Coeur d'Alene Airport practicing takeoffs, landings, and maneuvers. One Saturday I worked with Pearl on flights of five or six landings each when I decided to send her out for solo practice. I sat down to watch on a bale of fresh-mown hay next to the runway. Pearl's first landing looked good. As she took off, I noticed a large four-engine plane approaching from the south, probably a DC-4. Pearl was landing on Runway 01—the correct one, according to wind direction. I watched as the U.S. Forest Service plane lined up for runway 32 when it suddenly dawned on me the two aircraft would cross paths.

A little nervous, I stood up. "Surely, Pearl will circle the airport while the other plane lands," I told myself. Instead she turned to base leg (right angle to the runway), then turned again to final approach, lining up with Runway 01. Covering my mouth, I watched while neither plane altered course, converging to a point like two lines in an angle. Pearl crossed in the DC-4's path with less than a hair to spare and landed in perfect form. Immensely relieved, I flagged her down and walked out to the plane. "Didn't you see that other airplane?"

"Yes," she answered, her chin set. "But I had the right-of-way!" No wonder I've been grey-haired since I was thirty. It's true; she did have the right-of-way. But who in her right mind, would stay on a path just to meet with a grizzly?

Not only was Pearl stubborn but outspoken too. Most students would rather die than let me know they had a problem. Not Pearl! Like everyone else she hated radioing the tower operators because they speak so fast. I generally have students first listen for one or two things—runways in use and/or area traffic. When they master that, then I add other information like wind direction and velocity. One day we decided to practice transmissions in the hangar on a 4-place, Piper Tri-Pacer with a good radio. Pearl pretended to call the tower, and I answered as the tower operator.

It wasn't long until she decided to fly. After rolling the airplane out the hangar and warming up the engine, Pearl took the mike and called the tower for taxi instructions. No one answered, so she tried again—still no answer. After the third try, I told her to turn on the radio. From the look on her face, you'd have thought it was the radio's fault. Pearl got her instructions and taxied to the end of the runway. She took-off and stayed in the traffic pattern as we planned to give her more radio experience by shooting landings. As she came downwind on her fourth approach, she called the tower. Apparently the garble confused her because she picked up the mike and said, "I'm not going to talk to you any more." She reached up and turned off the radio. I just loved that about Pearl. She'd say exactly what she thought, and her frustration would melt away.

Teaching Pearl radio communication seemed like child's play in comparison to navigation. She could identify any landmark on the aeronautical chart but just couldn't locate the same spot on the ground.

One evening we took a short cross country flight to St. Maries, then to Kellogg, and back to Coeur d'Alene. By the time we hit Kellogg, it was getting dark. Pearl figured her compass heading to Coeur d'Alene and took off. I knew she would hit the Air Terminal on the nose—I could already see the runway lights. To my surprise Pearl flew over the top of the airport and headed for Rathdrum. Having learned early in my career that mistakes teach more than verbal instruction, I held my tongue. Eventually she headed back to the Coeur d'Alene Airport, covering up with the comment, "Just wondered if we could see them play football from the air." She'd confused the high school's lighted football field with the airport.

We made another short flight a few weeks later to work more on Pearl's chart reading. She planned a course to Felts Field in Spokane, then to Deer Park airport and back to Coeur d'Alene. Flying like an old hand, Pearl didn't run into trouble until the last leg. As she started back to Coeur d'Alene, she didn't cross the foothills that run south of Mt. Spokane. Instead, she kept turning south, following the west side of the hills. When she reached Spokane Valley, instead of turning east toward Coeur d'Alene, Pearl turned west. I let her go until she approached the restricted area around Spokane Air Terminal. "Darn it!" she shouted when she figured out her location.

Pearl Mancheni following solo of Piper Tri-Pacer - 1971.

Sending Pearl on her long, solo, cross-country flight required a heap of faith on my part. Still, she needed to jump through that hoop to qualify for a Private Pilot Certificate. It worked out that Clay Henley's daughter, Robin, and another student were also ready for cross country flights. I decided to kill three birds with one stone, keeping an eye on Pearl and Robin while I flew a dual with the other student. Little did I know I would feel like a mother with three kids and only two arms.

I sent Pearl off, then Robin, and followed in a Cessna with my other student. Our first stop was to be Lewiston, ID. I could see Pearl ahead, right on course. Robin, however, started veering more and more to the left. I directed the student to fly in her direction, but by the time we reached her, Robin had corrected her direction. She later told me, "I just wanted to look at something."

Now I couldn't see Pearl. I fully expected we'd pick her up again in a few minutes, but we didn't. A couple of times I spotted an airplane ahead and below us, but in both cases they were crop dusters. I strained my eyes till they felt half out of their sockets, my imagination manufacturing crash scenes while my stomach turned flip flops. When we landed at the Lewiston airport, guess who was waiting at the gas pump. Pearl jerked open our door and said, "Where ya been? I've been waitin' half an hour."

While I taught Pearl to fly, she slowly recovered from surgery and chemo. For a few years she seemed her good old self, but we all knew she lived on borrowed time. Because of that, every outing seemed all the more special. I'd heard about a little landing strip at Horse Haven, in the mountains south of Pend Oreille Lake and east of Badger Mountain. The strip ran close to the north fork of the Coeur d'Alene River at the west base of Colt Mountain.

We planned to fly there one summer evening after work. I packed a picnic and stuck in a couple of books. With Pearl at the wheel, we took off at 4:30 in air smooth as glass. I immediately spotted Pend Oreille Lake to the north and not long after passing over Hudlow Saddle found the Horse Haven strip right below us. "That's an airport?" Pearl asked. "I can't land an airplane down there."

"Oh, yes you can," I replied. "It looks small cause we're so high."

"You fly," Pearl replied. "I don't feel so good." This was a typical reaction. Pearl wasn't about to admit she was scared. Wanting her to enjoy the trip, I took over, reducing the power some and starting a downward spiral. I planned my approach upstream and south of the strip, so I could maintain just enough power for airspeed. When I slipped around the end of Colt Mountain, we'd be there. If I overshot the strip, I wouldn't have enough horsepower to climb out of the rising terrain. Needless to say, timing was everything. Once we landed, we could see Horse Haven was like something from a fairy tale—a perfect getaway we could return to time after time in the next few years.

By now Pearl had practically become a family member. When I started flying balloons, Pearl was with me practically every flight. I had to be careful, though, as cancer had spread to her spine, and one hard landing could be crippling. I promised Gene, her husband, I would always be there when she flew, be it in a balloon or a plane. In spite of Pearl's illness she learned to fly solo in the Cessna 150 and 172, the Piper TriPacer and J3 Cub.

Our last carefree time together was in 1975 when we flew my TriPacer to L. A. to visit Disneyland. Like two little kids we hit every ride, every show, and practically every concession stand. Since uncooperative weather ruined our plans to go soaring at Elsenor, California, we decided to head to Las Vegas. After loading our luggage, Pearl climbed aboard the Tri-Pacer, and I started my preflight check. The right flap refused to retract. The mechanic we rounded up told us, "I can't fix it, but I can wire it in the up position, so you can still fly."

A bit frustrated, I took off, heading east, and got lost almost immediately because of low cloud ceiling and unfamiliar terrain. Finally I followed an airplane to a small airport, landed, but could find no one to help us, so finally circled back up through a break in the overcast where at last I got my bearings. Unable to land at Las Vegas International as I needed a transponder in the Tri-Pacer, we put down at an airport seventeen miles out and paid an outrageous price for a taxi to town. Although we had tickets to see Liberace, Pearl felt too sick and just wanted to go home.

Pearl died ten years after her initial diagnosis for cancer. The first woman certificated at Henley's Aerodrome's FFA-approved flight school, Pearl received her Private Pilot Certificate December 11, 1973. Losing my best friend was rough; she had stood by me through the toughest years of my life.

Chapter 17: Back to Instructing

"Let's rent a hangar at the Coeur d'Alene Air Terminal," Herb suggested one day many years after we had moved to Wolf Lodge. "Sure. Why not?" I answered with a little thrill of excitement that surprised me.

It took a long time after the war before I could enjoy flying again. Nearly every day I flew an airplane Herb repaired from Wolf Lodge back to its owner, but I wanted nothing to do with flying for hire. When I later finished nursing school and began working at Kootenai Memorial, more and more people asked me to teach them—maybe word leaked out when I started training Pearl. Also Kelly, now 16, wanted to learn and needed an activity to keep him occupied.

Clay Henley, who frequently phoned us from his home in Kellogg, Idaho, must have moved quickly when Herb told him of our plans. The next weekend when we drove to our hangar, Clay met us outside. "Meet your new neighbor!" he said. "I just rented the hangar next to you." So began my renewed love affair with the air and with teaching. I flew students after work at the hospital and on weekends and taught ground school one night a week at Coeur d'Alene Airways.

Most educators will agree instructing is a real learning experience-for the teacher. Although it didn't sink in for a long time, I now realize I got my first taste of teaching in the sixth grade. Mrs. Campbell, trying to keep me out of trouble, asked me to coach the fifth grade baseball team. I had those kids hitting, catching, pitching and fielding balls every minute they weren't in class, and for the first time in my life, I felt worthy and needed. Since then in spite of interludes and distractions, I seem to inevitably end back in teaching.

Through the years, I've figured out how students learn best. One can lecture all day about a maneuver or procedure, but students don't really understand until they execute it in flight. In spite of some raised eyebrows, I always let brand-new students fly from the moment we lift off. I spend fifteen to thirty minutes on the ground, having them taxi and steer with their feet. Then I immediately reinforce this during takeoff by asking them to leave their hands on the throttle and stick and their feet on the rudder peddles while I fly. Once we leave the traffic area, the students fly the airplane themselves while I give them verbal cues. If I want to demonstrate a maneuver, I'll take over and have students stay on the controls to feel what I'm doing. This system seems to work well

By the middle of the war, I felt confident I could teach most anyone with some ability to fly. Of the thirty seven instructors working for Buroker/Hicks, only one besides myself planned to stay with teaching. This must be why my colleagues asked me to troubleshoot their primary students. I loved the challenge and found most problems—nearly always difficulty with landing or coordination— easily corrected.

On landings most students look too close to the airplane when judging the distance to the runway. Instead, they need to look several hundred feet ahead which gives them time to plan their landing, much like looking at a road sign before getting to it. Coordination problems usually occur when students, holding the stick with their right hand, allow the stick to settle slightly to the right, causing the right wing to drop slightly. On the landing approach, novices (attempting to line up with the runway with the low wing) will apply opposite rudder and slip while landing. This situation accounts for many of those not-so-famous ground loops.

One unusual problem I solved involved my brother George who had been assigned to our school in 1943 by the War Training Service. "George flies just fine," his instructor told me, " but can't seem to handle the plane on the ground. Will you see if you can figure out what's wrong?"

Puzzled, I climbed aboard the J3 Cub with George in the rear pilot seat and me in front. Since I couldn't see him, I had to feel his actions by touching the rudder peddles. I could tell once we took off he could execute maneuvers very well. But when we landed, we wove back and forth dangerously while slowing to a stop. Since I could feel the peddle, I immediately recognized the problem. When George used one peddle, he had to slide his 5' 2" frame sideways, lifting his other foot off the other. He simply couldn't reach both.

"Taxi up to the service center," I told him. I jumped out, grabbed a cushion, and pushed it behind his back, checking his ability to now control the pedals. I made one landing with him, then sent him off on his first solo flight. George completed his primary, secondary, cross-country and flight instructor ratings, teaching for Johnson Flying Service in Missoula, MO, during the war and later working for the Civil Aeronautics Authority in Maui, Hawaii.

Another unusual situation developed during the war while I taught Warren Keating, a primary student. Warren had completed seven of the eight hours of instruction required before soloing. I had him practicing landings during the last thirty minutes of his eighth hour when I noticed that one landing seemed a bit shaky. On the next landing, he veered to the right, executing a beautiful ground loop (if you can call a ground loop beautiful).

The Cubs have an awkward setup which forces the pilot to use the rudder peddles with his toes and the brakes with his heels. When we quit spinning, I discovered Warren's heel jammed on the brake, wedging the rudder peddle in full right position. He actually had to remove his foot from the shoe before we could pry the shoe loose. Knowing Warren felt terrible about not soloing, I suggested he remove his other shoe. Shoving them both in the baggage compartment, I asked if he could fly in his socks. "Sure I can," came the answer, after which he shot three perfect solo landings—in his stocking feet.

If Warren's solo seemed unusual, so did Fred Murphy's, a local tugboat operator whose towing and piling business had slacked off during winter. The weather that winter was good on many days, but on others it was totally unsuitable for flying. Fred, taking to the air right from the start, was a fun student to teach in spite of frosty conditions. The day I planned to solo him, though, the snow started falling. I felt nervous; the visibility wasn't too bad, but snow, like rain, is unpredictable. When Fred told me he still wanted to fly in spite of my misgivings, we warmed up the engine and took off. Before long, I got out and let him make three solo landings. Over the years whenever I ran into Fred, I had to wait while he told his cronies the story of me soloing him in a snow storm.

Although Fred and Warren's solos have stuck in my mind, undoubtedly my most memorable student is Bill, a middle-aged man with a grown son who could fly. One of a kind, Bill knew all about flying before his first lesson. In fact he knew the answers before I asked the questions. I guess he figured spending all his spare time at Henley Aerodrome, drinking coffee and hangar flying gave him all the know-how he needed.

Generally , I would cancel flights in nasty weather conditions, especially with inexperienced students. Not with Bill. Even when instructors didn't fly, Bill insisted on going up. To keep him happy, I'd take him flying but wouldn't give him the controls, repeatedly explaining if he continued this, he'd end up with an empty wallet and stack up fifty hours before soloing. "I'm in no hurry," he'd reply. (Actually, he managed to solo in about thirty seven hours.)

When Bill progressed to cross country, I explained (though I don't think he listened) that we would first take a short, 150 mile flight to teach him to read charts, pick out landmarks, and locate and approach strange airports. Bill plotted his course from Henley Aerodrome to Sandpoint to Deer Park to Felts Field to Coeur d'Alene, then back to Henley.

Taking off, he flew up the valley to Sandpoint, approaching and landing according to the book. Before takeoff from Sandpoint I tried to give Bill some pointers. He wouldn't listen, saying, "I know this country!"

"Okay, old boy," I thought. "It's all right with me if we end up on the Pacific Coast." I figured it would be better for him to mess up today than on the day he soloed for cross country.

Bill took off from Sandpoint toward Deer Park about 30 degrees off course to the south. I started asking questions about things we could see. He always had an answer—always wrong. He paid no attention to his compass, even though I asked him occasionally about his heading. By now he had steered 90 degrees south of his plotted course and was turned around so badly we were headed back toward Henley. I asked Bill, "What lake's that?" knowing full well we were flying over his house in Spirit Lake. Looking at his chart, Bill replied, "That's Diamond lake" (which is in Washington). By the time he had veered 140 degrees off course and passed north of Henley in an easterly direction, Bill spotted Pend Oreille Lake and Farragut State Park with its big water towers left from the naval station built during the war.

"I can't believe this!" he sputtered, turning red. They say it's hard to teach an old dog new tricks, but Bill changed. From that day on he progressed and became a private pilot. When I see Bill now, we always laugh about his flight training.

Teaching guys like Bill just came with the territory, but teaching my own kids took on a whole new dimension. Of the three Sally posed the most challenge since she was terrified of airplanes, probably because of Herb's hair-raising hangar stories. When Sally married, her husband Dick wanted to fly in the worst way but insisted that Sally learn too. Sally finally agreed to try (just to appease Dick I always thought). They drove up from St. Maries once a week for ground school and then again on the weekends for flight lessons.

Sally...On Mom Teaching Her to Fly
What made me so afraid? When I was little, I rode my trike out on the apron where the planes gassed up. Neither Mom nor Dad gave many words of caution, so I'd get quite a ways out. I could never see the pilots cause they sit so low in the tail draggers. I guess I figured they couldn't see me either, so when they taxied in, I'd peddle that bike!

When I was in grade school, Dad would tell horrible stories like the one about a down draft that crashed a friend's plane against the mountains. They really scared me. Many times too I'd heard Grandma beg Uncle Cal not to race. Then, sure enough, I heard the phone ring one day and watched Grandma cry hysterically when she heard Cal was killed. After that, whenever Mom and Dad did aerobatics and stunt flying, my heart would jump into my throat—the two people I loved most were tumbling out-of-control in the sky.

It wasn't until I married Dick, and we had Anneliese and Katrina that Mom renewed her license to teach Kelly to fly. Kelly never really pursued it, but Dick said, "Boy, I'd sure like to learn." It wasn't long, though, before I felt pretty put out. While I packed diapers and formula and sat at the airport all weekend with the girls, Dick had a ball.

I'll have to admit it was out of spite that I decided to take flying lessons. If I couldn't have learned from Mother, I'd probably have never taken on the challenge. Now it was Dick's turn to watch the kids. Some days I had diarrhea so bad, we had to stop the plane three times. I was very, very apprehensive, but I'd made up my mind—I would master that machine.

I progressed at a snail's pace. A rough day bothered me. A windy day bothered me. Clouds just terrified me. But Mom just pushed ever-so-gently.

"Look! There's a few puffer bellies up here," she told me one day. "Let's fly through them." When we approached, my chest tightened. Then we flew into them, through them, and out with perfect ease. They ceased to be terrifying and became what they were—friendly, billowy clouds.

"I don't think mother's ever going to solo me," I grumbled to Dick. Believe it or not I had begun to feel impatient. Then one day at the Coeur d'Alene Airport, Mom and I had done a couple of touch and goes. "Okay, this time I want you to do a full stop," she instructed. "Taxi on over to the runway."

When she opened the door, I got chills. This was it. Filled with excitement and the fear of God, I prepared for takeoff. Unexpectedly a surge of confidence warmed me from head to toe; I knew I could do it. I took off, gripping the stick so tightly my sweaty hand kept slipping off. Nevertheless I went around, making three acceptable landings that filled me with pride. Totally exhausted, wonderfully exhilarated, I felt now I could do anything.

Sally's face when she climbed out of the plane after soloing beamed like I had never seen it beam. For years I had wanted to share my love for flying with her, yet I knew airplanes made her uncomfortable and frightened. That moment, I'm convinced, was one of the best in Sally's life. And seeing her conquer her worst fear made it one of the best for me too.

Along with those satisfying moments in teaching come some surprises and disappointments. A high school boy came to the airport with his father to see about learning to fly one weekend

Gladys and David Tate following his solo in Aeronca Champ - Nov. 17, 1980.

197

afternoon. "My schedule's full," I told them. "Another instructor could get you started."

"No! We came to see you. We want you," the father said. After they worked on me for a while, I agreed to put together a plan that fit his schooling and my schedule. David Tate was 17 years old. Since I find teaching new students easier if I know something about them, I asked "What school do you go to?"

"A church school," he said. "I run the printing press right now. Boy, I'll be glad when I get to do something else." That sounded strange, but I decided most school's have a newspaper. David soloed November 11, 1980, but never completed training for his Pilot Certificate. I forgot all about him until five years later when I opened the *Coeur d'Alene Press* to find him on the front page, holding a machine gun and wearing a T-shirt that said WHITE POWER. Apparently Missouri troopers made a routine traffic stop and discovered David driving a Chevrolet van stolen in Nevada. He killed one trooper and shot another policeman three times. I guess that boy who was tired of running the printing

Aryan Nation Complex, north of Hayden Lake, ID.

press advanced to more demanding activities. He and his parents were members of the Aryan Nations, a white supremacist group located a few miles north of Coeur d'Alene.

Another young man, Nick McCoy, came to me in 1980. He owned a Luscombe 8-A. A man of few words, Nick followed my instructions and spoke only when asked a question. Before students solo, the FAA requires instructors to teach all Federal Air Regulations. Early on I gave students a copy and explained they would be tested. Then I talked about regulations during flight lessons, so a formal test would not be required. Because of Nick's silence, I had a bad feeling. I made up a written examination on the FAR's (Federal Air Regulations) and asked him to take it one day in the flight office. He passed, but I filed it anyway.

I never saw Nick McCoy after the day I soloed him, but I had a feeling he might run into trouble. He owned an airplane and was flying in violation unless he had hired a new flight instructor. A newspaper later reported Nick flew into and damaged power lines near Rathdrum, Idaho, on February 15, 1985. Sometime later, he crashed in a farmer's field in deep snow and simply walked away never to return. Staff writer, Bill Morlin, in the March 4 *Spokesman-Review* stated, "Federal Authorities, in an ever-widening war against Neo-Nazis, are trying to ground the 'Aryan Air Force.' One of two planes in the squadron crashed in a farmer's hay field near Cheney last month, and the pilot was never located or identified."

A Seattle FAA attorney travelled to Coeur d'Alene to talk to me. I pulled Nick's test from the file as evidence that he had been tested on regulations, even though he had probably been flying illegally. Authorities never prosecuted since they couldn't prove Nick flew the plane. It still gives me the creeps to think I taught these young men to fly. One thing a teacher learns is that youth has many faces.

Chapter 18: Henley Aerodrome & the Good Ole' Days

Once I got back to instructing, my love of flying returned with a vengeance. Evenings, weekends, every minute not spent sleeping or working at the hospital, I spent flying or thinking about flying. Before long Herb and I felt uneasy at the Coeur d'Alene airport. Vandals had broken into Clay's hangar, and someone had punched holes through one of our TriPacer's wing fabric when we tied it down outside. We decided to move our three airplanes to Ross Point just east of Post Falls where George Neufeld had scraped a runway onto a bluff now known as Royal Highlands. Though not a place to solo students, this little runway did give them a feel for flying off a sod field.

All along Clay kept telling us, "We need an airport of our own where we can fun-fly." Herb and I liked the idea and started looking for a likely spot. Meanwhile Clay bought an English-built Tiger Moth. This two-place, open cockpit, bi-plane with a tail skid was built when airports had sod fields. Clay planned to

Gladys with Tiger Moth at Coeur d'Alene Air Terminal - 1972.

install brakes and replace the skid with a tail wheel, but he had to see it fly—NOW!!

"Come on...take it for a spin, Gladys," Clay said.

"I don't know," I replied. "It's been almost 40 years since I flew a no-brake plane." He didn't coax much before he talked me into it. I felt like a kid with a new toy but couldn't help wondering why Clay didn't fly it himself. After all, he handled a plane just a well as I. Later when Clay installed the brakes and tail wheel, I started checking out private and commercial pilots on the Moth. It seemed everyone except Clay wanted to take that antique for a spin.

We searched high and low for a potential airport to house our toys. Finally, the summer of 1972 we bought 80 acres 17 miles north of Coeur d'Alene on Highway 95. With our old Farmall tractor, we bladed off the young pine trees and soon had a strip. Both families spent hours cleaning up the area, staking out a picnic site, and having more fun than a bunch of prairie dogs.

By summer's end Clay had sprouted an idea that just wouldn't quit growing. He wanted in the worst way to open a general aviation airport

Clay Henley - 1972.

201

around the theme of a WWI English aerodrome. "To make the picture complete," he told Herb and I, "we're also going to need a hot air balloon." Try as he might to talk us into a partnership, Herb and I had no desire to operate another flight school. It just wasn't realistic for Herb at 78 to take on another big project. We decided instead to incorporate. Clay, the major stockholder, bought back ten acres for a flight school, and we called the original 80 acres Henley Aerodrome. At the same time we signed papers for the land, Herb and I put our home at Wolf Lodge up for sale, planning as were the Henleys to build on our new property.

One evening Clay, Nadine, Herb and I decided to visit Mark Semich, a young man who was manufacturing Semco balloons at his shop at Fernan Lake in Coeur d'Alene. Maybe Clay had this all planned, but before we left Semco, Clay had told Mark he'd buy a three-place balloon called a Challenger. From there we headed to a coffee shop to hash over the merits of the balloon.

Herb's spoke up first. "Who's going to fly the darned thing?" We all looked at each other. I waited the appropriate 20 seconds for Clay to say something, but he didn't.

"I will," I blurted out, having wanted to give ballooning a try ever since my cross-country motorcycle ride forty years before. No one argued, so I put away my anticipation for late summer when the balloon would be delivered.

As I was leaving for work at Kootenai Memorial Hospital one morning not long after, Herb grabbed me for his good-bye kiss. "After work let's fly the Pacer to Felts Field to pick up radio parts for the Stinson."

"Sounds good," I said, happy to oblige. "See you round 3:30." Back from Felts by 5:00, we rolled the Pacer into the hangar, then headed to Kootenai to pick up Herb's car. The flight had been companionable and the afternoon light beautiful. About a mile from the hospital, Herb, who was in the passenger seat, started trembling uncontrollably, startling me so much I nearly ran off the road. Just as quickly, he snapped out of it, shaking his head. "What happened?" he asked.

"Are you cold?"

"No. I just seemed to lose control." Grateful we were headed toward the hospital, I tried to stay calm. Granted, Herb had reached his seventies, but he seemed so healthy, so indestructible. A minute later, his body started shaking once again. "We're almost to the hospital," I told him, gripping his hand tightly with my free one. "A doctor will check you over."

"No way," he shouted, almost irrational. "I'm going home and lay down." I parked close to the emergency entrance to see what he'd say. Herb just sat there like the mannequin we used in nurses' training. When he started shaking the third time, I drove to the emergency door. "Bring a gurney," I shouted to the staff. Protesting, Herb was coaxed onto the cart, then examined by Dr. Daugharty who gave him a shot.

Within 30 minutes, Herb seemed his old self again, though a little shaken. "I want to admit you to run some tests," the doctor told Herb who reluctantly agreed. While the office processed Herb's paper work, I phoned Sally in St. Maries. "He seems fine now," I told her.

"I don't care," she answered. "I'm coming." As an afterthought she asked, "Are you calling Linda and Kelly?"

"They have so far to drive," I replied. "Let's see how he feels in the morning."

Linda's Account of Subsequent Events

Sally called and said Dad had sort of passed out and been admitted into the hospital for tests. The doctors didn't know the cause and didn't want him flying or driving in the event of a blackout. "I know it's really dumb to call you cause it's no big deal," Sally said, "but I thought you'd like to know because of your nightmares."

I hung up the phone, deeply disturbed. Sally knew about the reoccurring dream that tormented me since I moved to Yakima. In the dream Dad would be in a coma. Desperate, I'd try to wake him, but it was too late. I would wake in tears

and with a feeling of impending doom. After several horrible episodes, I told Sally about the nightmare and how nervous I felt. "Well, it's probably because you've never been as close as you'd like with Dad," she said. "Maybe you're wishing you could sit down with him and really talk." When I visited home, I tried to approach Dad after my conversation with Sally, but it just never worked. Too many people or kids would always be around.

I thought about Dad laying in the hospital. Then I got in my car, drove to work and for the first and only time lied to my boss. "My father's seriously ill," I told him. "I need to go to Spokane." When I walked into Dad's hospital room, he was up talking to everybody. "What are YOU doing here?" he asked.

"I just wanted an excuse to get off work for a couple of days—so get off my case!"

"Okay," he said, backing off.

While Mom and Sally went home to rest that afternoon, I visited with Dad.

The nightmare evaporated as my deepest wish came true; we talked like never before. A couple of hours later, I kissed Dad good-bye. He slipped into a coma that night from which he never awoke.

I sat by Herb's bed till the end, holding his hand and talking. He never spoke, never moved, but I rattled on and on just in case he could hear. I think I would have camped there the rest of my life if it would have helped.

Herb died May 22, 1973. His last breath came and went with little fanfare. "Breathe, Herb, breathe!" I insisted, willing him to live, but he left quietly like the gentle man he was. I felt as if someone had reached down my throat and ripped out my heart. What should I do? How could I live? The autopsy showed Herb's stomach was full of cancer but listed a series of strokes as the cause of death. Ironically, Herb had emerged from ulcer surgery just a year before with a clean bill of health.

I felt suspended in a glass bottle after Herb's death while the minutes ticked away. Detached, almost numb, I went through the motions of arranging a military funeral as Herb was a Navy veteran. When the buglers played taps at the cemetery, though, my heart broke and the flood gates opened. I ran off unable to talk to anyone. By the time I got home and the family gathered in, I had somewhat controlled my emotions, although I desperately longed to be alone. I went to work the next day and continued for the next seven years.

After losing Herb, I lost interest in everything—flying, the new air strip, building a home. I kept my job to keep from going crazy but would have never moved had our real estate agent not sold the farm. Reluctantly, I found an apartment in Coeur d'Alene until the house could be built, flying students in the evenings and passenger flights in the Tiger Moth on weekends. Pearl dropped by all the time to cheer me up (without her I don't know what I would have done), and every so often we'd check the progress on Clay's hot air balloon. I suppose that helped some, but the winter of '73/74 turned into worst of my life; depression enveloped me like the cloud cover often locked-in over Northern Idaho.

In spite of my despair, life went on. The contractor for Henley started digging a well in April 1973, a month before Herb's death but didn't locate an adequate water supply until February 2, 1974, after drilling seven times. Even then, we had to put in an underground storage tank of 8,000 gallons and limit it to domestic use.

Clay started his flight school, Henley Aircraft Company, with a pair of Tiger Moths and a covey of J-3 Cubs. He also made the smartest deal he ever made by luring Walt (Whimpy) Redfern from Tekoa, WA, to take up residence at the aerodrome. Today Walt has an international reputation for his superior craftsmanship in replicating vintage aircraft. His first undertaking, while still in Tekoa, was to build a Night Twister B1 with a 15' wing span. He has since built a Great Lakes Bi-Plane, Starduster Two, five

German Fokker DR-1 Tri-Planes, a French Nieuport Bi-Plane, Sopwith Camel Bi-Plane, and English DH-2. He also worked with Bob Sleep in building his famous Albatross, signing off the work as required by the FAA. The Albatross now sits in a museum in Huntsville, Alabama.

I don't believe there's a better "grape vine" than that connected with aviation. Everyone heard about Clay's aerodrome, Redfern's arrival, the balloon—all of it. Before we could even fly in our Cubs, enthusiasts buzzed our property to check out the site. Even as we prepared the landing strip for surfacing, three planes landed in May 1973: Wayne Anderson in a Piper J-3, Gene Soper in a Duncan Sport, and Skeeter Carlson in a Pussmoth. By June the Wingover Cafe opened, soon followed by the hangar.

Henley Aerodrome, a base for vintage airplanes, held dedication ceremonies July 9, 1973—in memory of Herb Buroker and Cal Dawson, both flying companions of Clay Henley. Included in the dedication was a speech by Darrell Manning, Idaho, Director of Aeronautics, and the landing of ten parachutists on the field. To top off the ceremony members of the West Coast Scarf and Goggle Club took off from Henley in vintage aircraft for a cross-country tour. Over the next few years Clay built up a small museum of classic planes that drew aviators like flies: a Fokker DR-1 Tri-Plane, French Nieuport Bi-Plane, Sopwith Camel, two Tiger Moth Bi-Planes, and a French Stompe Bi-Plane.

Numerous air shows featuring antiques aircraft as well as other attractions brought large crowds to Henley during good-weather months. Dr. Dave Rahm in his Bucker-Jungmann, a pre-World War II German BiPlane, quickly became the main attraction. A geology professor from Western Washington College in Bellingham, Dave always opted to spend his summer weekends at Henley if he wasn't booked somewhere else. The featured performer at an International Air Show in Abbotsford, B.C., Dave so impressed King Hussein of Jordan who watched from the grandstand that Hussein asked Dave to perform for the Jordanians.

After that show, the king asked him to stay and train a Jordanian aerobatic team with the assistance of Dave's friend, Steve Wolf. Before they got back home, though, Dave crashed August 1976 while staging another special show for Hussein. The news just crushed those of us at home. They didn't come any nicer than Dave.

Returning to the States, Steve and his wife, Liz, moved to Northern Idaho. Although he was a talented pilot, Steve was even more talented in aircraft design, building a one-of-a-kind biplane he named the Sampson, powered with a 450 hp Pratt and Whitney engine. On August 1, 1985, Steve zoomed to 10,000 feet in less than 4 minutes in his craft—a new world record that was timed and verified at the National Air Meet at Oshkosh, Wisconsin.

Henley Aerodrome probably drew the Dave Rahms and Steve Wolfs because of Clay—a truly colorful character. Even more handsome at fifty than at twenty, Clay always wore a cowboy hat over his silver-streaked hair, kept a loaded rifle in his truck and a handgun in one of his boots. Fond of his liquor, Clay would sometimes go on a toot which could last all night or several days. When anyone tried to talk him out of drinking, he would just smile his silly grin and drink up.

Henley Aerodrome, Athol, ID - 1973.

One morning, Walt Redfern went to the Wing Over Cafe for a cup of coffee. Finding Clay in a booth, Walt joined him. "See that sugar bowl over there?" Clay told Walt after a minute.

"Yeah," Walt responded, spying it across the room not far from a foursome eating breakfast. Clay took a gun from his pocket, aimed at the bowl, and blasted the thing to kingdom come.

"Give me that gun," Walt demanded. Clay laughed and handed him the gun, then reached in his pocket and pulled out another. Walt confiscated four guns in all. Needless to say, the customers having had breakfast left quickly. "I threw some money on the table," one man said timidly to anyone who would listen. "Hope it's enough." Clay loved airplanes, guns and liquor, though not necessarily in that order.

When sober, one of Clay's favorite tricks was to run "dawn patrol." Too frequently he would shanghai a couple of pilots and buzz the aerodrome houses until the occupants gave up and crawled out of bed. But odd as it seemed, Clay never flew alone and later refused to fly at all.

Because of Clay's personality, it's easy to see how some pilots forgot safety. This madhouse wasn't exactly what I had in mind

Gladys and Fokker DR I Tri-plane at Henley Aerodrome.

when we talked about a fun place to fly.

Since Clay had not installed a radio on the field, only safety-minded pilots would call in to give their position, altitude and intentions, so other aircraft in the area would know they had company. It seemed that half or more of the planes landing at Henley made down-wind approaches over the airstrip, peeling off at mid-runway like military fighters only to turn 180-degree into the wind and land. That really meant danger for anyone making a normal landing in accordance with Civil Air Regulations.

The FAA officials, not wanting to file a violation, told Clay he needed to maintain better control, I bet they found him easy to approach, and I'm sure they left feeling pretty good. I doubt they would have appreciated his solution. Clay had previously

Clay Henley, Gladys and Dave Rahm at Henley Aerodrome.

put up a string of flag poles from the cafe to the flight office with flags of the United States, Canada, Idaho, Germany, New Zealand and Australia. After the officials left, he just added another pole with a red flag. "This is the FAA flag," he told everyone. "Any time a member of the FAA is on the field, we'll run up this flag. If you're on your way in, make a normal approach—NO BUZZING!"

Not long after Clay installed the red flag, another dangerous fad began. A large flag pole stood between the Wingover Cafe and the highway. Joe Watts, while approaching to land in the Travel Air 4,000 decided to make his down-wing leg between the cafe and flag pole below the roof of the cafe. He created quite a stir. Soon it seemed like every pilot worth his salt wanted to match Joe's feat.

I'll admit this was fun, but we thought only of ourselves. We were pilots who had years of flying under our belts. I knew it was just a matter of time before someone got hurt. Ken Zachary, just 18 years old, decided to show off his skill while flying a group of jumpers at a Henley airshow one weekend. An above-

Steve Wolf and Samson - 1988.

average student, Ken had just passed his commercial and multi-engine certificate. Sally and Kelly were helping at the ticket gate when Kelly spied Ken about 10 feet off the ground, heading between the flag pole and the cafe. Thank goodness Sally hit the ground; she could have been smashed to pieces. I got pretty steamed about that one.

I argued frequently with Clay about these dangerous antics. By the time I'd get home from work the next day, though, I'd

Steve Wolf, Gladys Buroker and Walt (Whimpy) Redfern and Samson.

usually find a note in my mail box with an apology or a gift. Pearl came home with me after work one evening to do some flying. Walking to the hangar with my favorite white helmet and goggles (I never let them out of my sight), I ran into Clay with whom I battled the day before.

"Where'd you get the helmet and goggles?" he asked.

"A very good friend of mine gave them to me."

"And don't you forget it!" he laughed, giving me a hug.

When we got inside, Pearl said, "You guys almost made me cry." I guess you could say Clay was like a brother.

Those carefree days came to an abrupt halt. Clay's son, Randy Henley, an Air Force fighter pilot, flew in to spend a week's leave with his dad on January 9, 1977. Half an hour after I left Randy's welcome-home party at the Wing Over (about 10:00 p.m.), someone pounded violently on my door. "Clay needs help! We think it's a heart attack." Clay's words to me when I decided on nursing rushed back: "Learn that stuff good," he said. "I'll need your help someday."

I hurried to the cafe to find Clay flat on his back surrounded by his hysterical family trying to assist him. Performing CPR while we waited for the ambulance, I could feel him slipping away. "Why can't I save him now that he needs me?" I thought desperately. Clay died in transit to Kootenai Memorial Hospital.

Nadine revealed in later conversations that Clay had heart trouble for some time which explained why he grounded himself—his friends had puzzled over that for years. By creating Henley Aerodrome, Clay created an environment where he could still be immersed in flying. Nothing was more beautiful to him than pilots executing precision aerobatics, skydivers knifing their way to earth, and balloons and gliders riding the breeze on warm, summer evenings.

Life went on without Herb and Clay, but their deaths marked a new era in my life. For ten years in my late middle age I had returned to teaching, had learned to fly jump planes and glide, and had mastered the fine art of ballooning.

Chapter 19: Ballooning: Do You Know Where You're Going?

Ballooning brought me back from terrible depression during those early Henley years. After Herb died, my family and friends thought I'd never emerge from my black hole. I helped dedicate Henley Aerodrome in July. I went to work. I taught flying. I saw Clay and my other friends. But I felt old and helpless at age fifty eight? until the phone rang one day in early August of 1972.

"She passed inspection," Mark Semich told me. "The FAA gave the Challenger an ATC (Approved Type Certification)." The first of the Challenger models, the TC-7 (650 lb. pay load AX7) came equipped with three burners and a wicker basket for only $6,795. Clay had paid $3397 down a year before when he ordered the balloon but came up short on delivery. I wanted the balloon badly—I needed a lift—so paid the balance and agreed to turn over all revenue to Clay until he was paid off.

Mark agreed with Clay to teach an aeronaut (a balloon flyer), which he emphasized he did not ordinarily do. Believe me, he meant it. Mark gave me one 30 minute lesson on using the burner while his son tethered, or anchored, the 75,750 cubic foot balloon with a rope. He also provided three free flight lessons, all with a slight southwesterly breeze, for a total of two hours and forty minutes, commenting for about fifteen seconds on how to handle high speed landings. "Good grief," I thought. "What do I do in a strong wind?" Then he instructed me to take my ten minute solo flight. That was it, less than four hours and I'm supposed to take a flight test.

"I'll make arrangements with Del Randels, the FAA Inspector, for your flight test," Mark told me, anxious to be on his way. August wind conditions took a turn for the worse as I waited eagerly to fly my new toy. Finally Mark called. "Plan to lift off at 4 p.m. from the rest stop west of Coeur d'Alene."

Having flown all day at Henley, I told Mark we should

consider changing our launch site. "If we take off from here, the wind might take us right over Lake Coeur d'Alene."

"Just go a little higher, and you'll pick up a south wind," he answered.

"But I've been flying all day. Wind's from the north."

"Go up to 3,000 feet, and you'll have a south wind," he said wearily.

With Del in the basket, I reluctantly went through the preliminaries and inflated the balloon. We lifted off, immediately heading southeast toward the lake.

Mark Semich and Gladys in Semco 9GB.

"I'll go up to 3,000 feet," I told Del. We experienced no change at 3,000, so we lifted to 4,000. The thrill of ballooning comes from knowing that though you can play a little with the wind, more often it plays with you. Because of this, aeronauts need to be careful, a lesson Mark hadn't yet learned.

"I don't think we'll get a wind change no matter how high we go," I said.

"I agree," Del answered. "Maybe we oughta land before we get to the lake." Picking the only field between the water and us, I turned down the heater jets and began my approach. The ground crew (Mark, Sally, Dick and the two girls), sped up in their vehicles and waved us off. "Don't land," we heard faintly from below. "Wires."

I hastily reopened the burners and sailed over the water. The wind diminished as we moved south at a snail's pace, the tin foil lake reflecting blue sky and mountains that looked cut from black poster board. Del and I settled back to swap hangar stories until the first of two propane tanks suddenly emptied. "Wonder how we're gonna keep our feet dry," I commented, sobering a little. By 8:30 p.m. the red and orange light show blazed on the western horizon.

I suggested we go higher as we might catch enough breeze and make it across the lake to some fields on the east side. Del wanted to stay low and land along the shore. "Remember, Gladys," he said, "the balloon will sink like a rock. We don't have life jackets." Just then we noticed a small boat speeding toward us. When it got close enough, Del hollered, "If we drop you a rope, will you tow us to the dock?" We could see one in the distance.

"Sure!" the driver said, happy to be part of the action. We dropped a rope which he handed to a young girl next to him. Then he opened the throttle, ripping the rope through her hands. Good thing she let go-besides rope burns, she would have taken a swim. The driver circled around for another try. "Go slower," Del told him. "This balloon weighs a lot!" This time it worked.

When I hollered, "Drop the rope," the air moved just enough to set the basket on the dock. I released the hot air, collapsing the envelope on the beach. What a relief!

"Why don't you see if you can find a phone and call Mark," Del suggested. "I'll get the balloon ready to haul." I climbed the steep bank to the road and found a telephone at the second house. Then I trudged back through the weeds, only to find several men lifting the basket packed with gas tanks and envelope onto a large boat that looked more like a yacht. "This guy saw us and came to investigate," Del told me. "Said he'd take us to Coeur d'Alene since he's headed that way." We were both relieved. Hauling that balloon up the bank would have been a real job.

I boarded the craft and went below to wash before meeting our patron. Imagine my surprise to find Jim Cully at the helm, a man I'd taught to fly in the 40's. "Except for the hair, you haven't changed much, Gladys," he said, giving me a bear hug. Jim helped us unload at the Coeur d'Alene dock and pulled away just as

Gladys and Clay Henley at Henley Aerodrome.

216

Mark pulled up. No doubt he felt a little cantankerous, having navigated nearly every back road in Kootenai County trying to find us. Then seeing us just as we were pulling away from the dock. Even so, he helped us load the Challenger into his pickup.

Del turned to me. "No question about you passing the test," he said. "We'll just have to find somewhere to do the paper work."

"I know just the place," Mark spoke up. He drove us to the Back Door, a restaurant/bar on Appleway. Thirsty for a cold beer, I followed Mark and Del into the bar where an obviously frustrated Sally and Dick found us around eleven p.m. That night I received my Hot Air Balloon Rating and became the first woman in the Northwest to qualify as a balloon aeronaut.

A few weeks after our flight, I ran into Del Randels at Henley on one of his routine visits. "Just got a letter from my boss in Oklahoma City," he told me. "He wants to know why it took ten hours to give a young lady a flight test. And you know what?" he continued. "My wife asked the same question."

Within weeks I picked up more balloon students than I could handle. To my surprise, though, I generated even more income from selling night rides at Henley. Lit up like a giant light bulb against the black sky, the red, white, and blue Challenger, stopped Highway 95 traffic coming and going. Drivers would stop to watch which was guaranteed to lure in a few for a ride. The crew and I tethered the ropes to two cars, so the balloon would stay put. Then we'd take on two passengers at a time, warning them to stay in the basket until secured by the ground crew; otherwise, the balloon would break free due to weight loss.

One night a group of military officers, camping at nearby Farragut State Park, spied the balloon and drove in for a ride. In lively spirits from drinking a few beers, they were primed for a few good laughs. Each time I landed a pair, I warned them to stay in the basket. After several successful rounds, pandemonium struck. On landing, one young man, preoccupied with shouting to his buddies on the ground, apparently missed my warning. To my surprise, he climbed over the side and jumped the last two or three feet.

Gladys and Pearl Mancheni landing, following a flight for cancer. Somewhere northwest of Spokane.

The balloon shot up with such force it snapped the tether like a string. "No!" I shouted, hanging on. Not many things are more dangerous than free-flying in the dark. The officer still aboard sobered up fast. While the balloon drifted north toward blackness, I quickly opened the side vent, hoping that would let us down before we left the airport. Meanwhile, I handed the officer a rope secured to the basket. "If the ground crew catches up," I told him, "drop the rope." As it turned out, we landed just before reaching Highway 95.

Adventures like this thrilled Clay. The fact I had paid him back his investment didn't keep his dirty mitts off the Challenger for one minute. Every morning, as soon as I'd leave for the hospital, he'd have his crew get it out. To my knowledge they never free-flew the balloon, but they frequently damaged the envelope inflating it. I found so many burn holes that I finally bought a commercial sewing machine to make repairs with time I didn't have. Every once in a while I'd tear into Clay, but I could never stay mad for long.

I taught many students in the four years I owned the Challenger. Thank goodness my first was a family member. One morning, Dick and I lifted off from Henley just as the sun cleared Bernard Peak. Drifting south, we anticipated a lazy, uneventful flight until I noticed our speed increasing as we passed over the Louisiana Pacific Mill and angled across Highway 95. Glancing back at the mill's smokestack, I caught my breath— grey plumes of smoke blew horizontally to the south. Dick realized we'd picked up a brisk breeze. "Think we should look for a field?" he asked. "Yeah," I answered uneasily.

Now over the Rimrock, bordering Hayden Lake on the north, we could see only one field before water. I tried desperately to recall what Mark told me about high speed landings. As we approached, I briefed Dick: "Instead of touching down and deflating, we'll pull the rip cord five to ten feet up, opening the envelope's apex. That'll let out the air and lay the basket on its side." I didn't mention the down side to my strategy.

Preparing to descend, I said, "You pull the rip cord when I say, and I'll handle the burner." Clearing the fence by several feet, I yelled, "Pull!" We hit hard, throwing Dick out of the basket ahead of the burner. Just then the wind chose to drag the balloon and basket toward Dick's elevated backside while he scrambled for his life on all fours. This was definitely funnier than any Abbot and Costello routine I'd ever seen; I thought I'd die laughing. But when Dick walked stiffly back to the basket, he didn't even crack a smile. I guess I didn't earn any good mother-in-law points that day.

I just began to feel safe as an aeronaut when a memorable Walla Walla, WA, couple, Nat and Ginger Vale, and their friend, Bill Lloyd, began lessons. Soloing quickly, the men talked me into sending the balloon to Walla Walla where I soloed Ginger a few weeks later. By May 1974 both the Vales and Lloyds purchased balloons in time to participate with me and two other aeronauts in the opening ceremonies of the Spokane World's Fair.

Opening day at World's Fair. Gladys and crew fight wind while inflating balloon - 1974.

220

Little did I know these three would later organize the Walla Walla Stampede, the largest balloon meet in the Northwest, attracting an amazing 58 balloons in 1990.

Meets like the Stampede can't be equalled for beauty and companionship. Balloons dot the blue sky in every combination of vibrant colors—red, white, and blue, neon yellow, hot pink, and green—as they drift lazily with the wind. The participants welcome each other like old friends which is why Dick and Sally, Pearl and I, hit every balloon meet we could manage.

Our last in Mountain Home, Idaho, surpassed the rest for excitement. Sunday evening Dick and a buddy took the last flight, with the women following as ground crew. The balloon moseyed along the contour of the countryside, while the guys enjoyed the long, dusky shadows. Parked ahead of them in a field, we noticed the wind picking up and figured they'd land nearby. Sure enough, they began descending but were moving way too fast. When they hit ground, the basket kept going, quickly outdistancing Sally's and my puny legs. It blasted through a fence, skipped over a road and knocked down another fence like a row of toothpicks.

Opening day, Expo '74 WORLD FAIR, Spokane, WA. Balloons in background.

Just then a sightseer sped up in a jeep. "That balloon's in trouble," I hollered. "Can you stop it?" He shifted into first and took off fast, pulling dangerously close to the speeding basket. Ever-so-carefully, Dick pulled himself above the basket's edge and tossed the ground rope to the driver, yelling, "Tie this down if you can!" Somehow the man managed to pull the balloon to a halt. "What happened, Dick?" I asked, running to the balloon. Dick shrugged. Walking to the envelope's apex, he opened the deflation panel and found the rip cord mechanism jammed. Needless to say, Dick talked about his wild ride for some time to come.

When Clay died I wanted to keep the balloon but sold it after finding I could no longer depend on the ground crew. After it sat in a garage for two years, I sold it to an enthusiast who restored it and then signed up for lessons. One evening he and his instructor tried to outrun an incoming storm over Spokane. While they were setting down, a gust of wind tossed the basket to the ground, ejecting them both. About an hour later, a Northwest Airline pilot radioed Seattle Center, reporting a runaway balloon at about 22,000 feet.

I was saddened by the news that the Challenger crashed. The balloon taught me a lot about air currents—and relaxation. To this day I remember lifting off at Henley right before sundown, with a gentle southwesterly wind floating me at 1000 feet toward Lake Pend Oreille. As I approached the lake, I'd let down just close enough to the tree tops to pick up an offshore breeze to carry me back home. Now that's what I call living.

Chapter 20: Jump Flying and Gliding

About the same time I started ballooning, shortly after Henley Aircraft started business, a group of parachuters, dubbed the Henley Hummers, moved in. I still remember a few: Stephen Morrow, Tom Cannarozzo, Jan and Tom Sullivan, and Tim Flores. Since Clay had no space to store their gear, they eventually bought some property a few miles up the road at Athol airport, now known as Hackney Air Park. Morrow and Cannarozzo soon opened the Ozmo Para Center at Athol, advertising complete sky diving training, first jump courses, exhibition sky diving, parachute sales and service, and an FAA-certified rigger. Quite frequently Osmo Para Center called me to fly their jump planes.

Boy had things changed since I learned to skydive back in the '30's. In the typical jump plane, all seats except for the pilot's are removed to reduce the weight and allow jumpers more maneuverability. While the plane climbs to 9,000 feet, the jumpers sit on the floor. At altitude, they swing up a specially-designed door, attaching it to the wing at which point the lead jumper climbs onto a step clamped to the landing gear leg and then onto the plane's right wheel while the pilot applies the brakes. Holding the wing strut, the first jumper positions the other two on the step, so at the signal they can jump simultaneously.

I found flying first-time jumpers to be the most fun. They would complete their three-day ground instruction at Osmo and then take their first jump, free of charge. Regulations required the student to first complete three static jumps at 3,000 feet with the student's rip cord hooked to a cable secured to the fuselage. When students jumped, the cord automatically pulled, opening the chute and allowing them to experience falling and landing.

Then came the real thing. On the first run, the jump master (instructor) dropped a weighted streamer over the target to gauge when to put out the students, so they would hit the target. Trees surrounded Hackney airport, and occasionally students hit them, ripping their parachutes but seldom hurting themselves. On jump run the master positioned the students and then gave me instructions from the open door based on wind direction and velocity. When he liked the conditions, he yelled, "Jump."

Most students willingly stepped off the wheel. Others needed a little coaxing, so I'd ease off the brake to give them a boost. Nearly everyone's survival instincts would kick in at the last second, telling them, "DON'T LET GO!" and they'd struggle, white-fingered, to hang on. (I knew how they felt.) Then their hands would slip, and they'd drop while I'd bank steeply to the right to watch the chute inflate. Then I'd circle and climb for the next jump while the master observed his students' landings.

One day, the last student to jump didn't hesitate like many. He got out and jumped the second he heard the command. I made

Trio of jumpers at Henley Aerodrome. Cessna 182 jump plane in background.

my usual swing to the right and saw his open chute floating off to his side— unattached. The student fell like a rock as we watched in horror. "Pull your reserve. Pull your reserve," the jump master shouted although the boy couldn't hear. About that time, the reserve inflated. I tell you, that was enough excitement for a few days. Back on the ground, the jump master hurried to the student.

"What happened?"

"You said if our main chute malfunctioned to release it and open the reserve. I just wanted to see how it worked." Needless to say, the young man got an earful.

After flying jumpers for a few months, I came to appreciate how single-minded they could be. I taxied the Cessna 180 out to pick up a load of jumpers one weekend day when I noticed a man dressed in jump gear approaching the airplane on crutches. I figured he wanted to ask a question or chat for a minute. Instead, he handed his crutches to a buddy and proceeded to scoot on his rear into the airplane. "You gonna jump?" I asked in amazement?

He smiled and offered his hand. "Hi. I'm Dan Miller; it's just a broken leg."

"Now I've seen everything," I laughed. Even though I was concerned, I knew it was useless to say more. After all, hadn't I done some pretty crazy things? In no time we climbed to 10,000 feet. When I stalled, Dan calmly pulled himself to the door and jumped like he'd done it a million times. By the time I landed and taxied in, Dan was packing his chute for the next jump.

Another weekend, not much different than most, I jump flew ten veteran jumpers, who joked around, telling stories and ribbing each other as usual. On the last jump, I noticed a dense, black storm front approaching from the southwest. I'd never seen anything to match this. The fellows sat on the floor, cutting up when I interrupted them. "An ugly storm's approaching," I said

They didn't seem interested, but one fellow took a look. "Can we get to altitude before it gets here?" he asked.

"I think so," I answered, knowing it would be close. He sat

down, unconcerned. For the most part, parachuters are pretty pragmatic, and this group must have felt confident they could get down. As we flew, I thought about a story I'd heard from a fellow instructor, Joe Watts. He had been flying a group of parachuters to Reno over sagebrush country in a twin Beechcraft when Joe suddenly lost an engine. After attempting repeatedly to restart it, he turned to tell the guys to jump, but the airplane was already empty. These guys must have felt safer in their chutes than in the plane.

My thoughts returned abruptly to the situation at hand. "Almost to altitude, " I told the jumpers. The storm, nearly on us, contained no turbulence or moisture. "Weird," I thought.

Malfunction parachute jump, landed with reserve in a tree in Gladys' back yard - 1988.

"This isn't a dust storm—the color's wrong." With the jumpers out, I made my fastest descent ever, running into grey dust before I landed. As I secured the airplane, someone ran up to me. "Guess what," he shouted. "Mount St. Helen's erupted!" It took weeks to clean the area and months before nature absorbed the engine-choking fallout. What a mess!

With the number of jumpers and the danger involved, one would think injuries and fatalities would be common. Actually we lucked out with only a few close calls. One weekend while drinking coffee in the Wingover, I watched a team practicing eight-man jumps. I noticed the guys helping one of their friends into the classroom when someone burst through the door yelling, "Steve Morrow got hit in the last pattern. Can you look at him, Gladys?"

I found Steve on the couch, white as a ghost. He told me between short, fast breaths that a hot-dogger had hit him hard in the stomach with his hard hat shortly after they left the plane. In spite of the pain, Steve opened his chute but couldn't stand once he hit the ground. "Internal bleeding," I thought to myself as I ran for Pearl, who was spending the day with me. One look at Steve, and she said, "Get him to the hospital."

We helped Steve into the back seat of my car with Pearl holding his head in her lap. "Faster, Gladys, faster!" she shouted. I had already hit eighty. At the emergency room the doctor took one look. "Get him ready for surgery." Steve had ruptured his spleen and could have died.

Another day, Kelly and I watched a jump from my yard. I could see the Cessna but couldn't hear the engines. "What's going on?" I asked Kelly who could hear a little better.

"Uh oh," he said. "The props are stopped." We ran to the runway to watch the forced landing on Henley's 2,600 foot runway. Without the engines, the pilot had no hydraulic system which meant no landing gear or flaps. We held our breath as the Cessna put down, throwing up gravel and sparks as it careened wildly to a stop at the runway's end. Both propellers and the plane's belly suffered serious damage, but the pilot's reputation took the worst hit. He committed the unforgivable sin of running out of gas.

Twin engine Cessna's landing after running out of gas.

Considering the energy our parachuters devoted to their sport, it's not surprising Henley produced top notch teams. One of the best, Geronimo, had me fly them in a Cessna 182 while they practiced for the National Sky Diving Competition. Tim Flores, Jeff Wragg, Randy Hauck and Brad Dunkin won the 1976 nationals and took third in the world sky diving competition in Oudshan, South Africa, that same year. Another local team took nationals in 1977 and 1979.

Because of their success, parachuters flocked to Henley to rub elbows with the winners. In early summer of 1979, a four-man Canadian team decided to practice at Henley using Tim Flores's jump plane. Looking for publicity, they invited a *Coeur d'Alene Press* reporter to fly with them and get photos. I told him to sit on the floor with his back against the instrument panel to put him in the best position to shoot." When the door opens and they jump, I'll make a steep turn to the right." I said. "Snap your pictures then."

The reporter didn't say much on the way up. I figured he was eavesdropping, which, believe me, can be interesting with jumpers. When we reached altitude, I told the Canadians, "I'm starting jump run."

"Door open," the captain ordered, and an icy blast swooped through the cabin. At this point, I had to concentrate. "Five right," the captain directed as we approached the target, so I adjusted five-degrees, then reduced power and applied flaps, slowing to 65 mph and holding the right brake.

"All out," he said while I focused on compensating for the weight shift to the right. "Jump," the captain ordered.

"Take your pictures now," I told the reporter as I rolled to the right but he didn't move. Glancing over my shoulder, I recognized the signs of hyperterror—eyes locked straight ahead, body stiff. "You all right?" I asked. No answer. Landing with the door still open, I taxied onto the ramp and shut down the engine. Without saying "Thank you," "Good-bye," or "Go to hell!" the reporter climbed out and headed for his car. Two weeks later he returned to apologize. "I've never been so scared in my life," he said. "I knew I'd die when they opened the side of the airplane, and I looked down 10,000 feet."

My days were packed with nursing, teaching, ballooning, and flying jumpers. I didn't think I could squeeze in one more thing until I walked into the house one day to a ringing telephone. "Mrs. Buroker?" a deep voice said. "My name's Lee Fisher. I teach math at Central Washington College in Ellensberg, and I'm lookin' to get a balloon rating for my Commercial and Flight Instructor Certificate. How would you feel about instructing me in ballooning if I teach you gliding."

"Yes!" I said, not even pausing to think it over. By the time our conversation ended, we worked out a tentative agreement. I knew if I played my cards right, I'd soon be teaching gliding, but before I committed I ran our proposal by Clay. Pleased with the added attraction, he quickly approved our plan. Lee trailered his two-place Schweitzer 2-22 to Henley the summer of '74, assembling it in record time.

Clay installed a tow hitch on the Tiger Moth which Lee had never flown, so I agreed to check him out. On our first flight at about 2,000 feet, the Moth swallowed a valve, forcing a landing.

As I signaled the glider pilot to release, I could hear Lee yelling, "I've got it." That was typical Lee — always in charge. As pilot in command, I yelled back, "No way," although I could feel him on the controls all the way down. I needed to get a few things clear.

"I've flown that Moth for hundreds of hours, Lee. I'm the one who makes the decisions!"

"Yeah, yeah—okay," he agreed grudgingly.

Some of us didn't want to stop learning on the glider just because the Moth was down, so in the meantime we asked Lee to teach us ground launching. He agreed but told us he'd need a powerful pickup which a student quickly volunteered. In no time we were ground launching on the Coeur d'Alene Air Terminal's mile-long runways.

Within two weeks we completed our respective ratings, and I began training the growing list of aviators anxious to master gliding. Always reluctant to take the controls if my student could handle the situation, I made a mistake one day in a glider that could have cost someone his life. A new student had just lifted off, when he started climbing much too steeply. "Level off!" I said quickly. Perhaps I should have taken the controls for takeoff.

Schweitzer 2-22 at Henley Aerodrome.

No sooner did I say that than the tow rope broke. It's a good thing it did as we could have lifted the plane's tail and sent the tow pilot into a dive. I grabbed the controls and pushed the nose down, struggling to maintain speed for the 180-degree turn and down-wind landing at the airport which though wobbly was successful.

Another experience (some may call it thrill) was flying with commercial pilot Dick LaBute who wanted a glider rating. During an advanced lesson, I planned for him to box-the-wake while being towed. The air flow from a plane's engines creates a wake similar to that of boat in water. To box-the-wake the glider pilot crosses to the right of the wake, drops down beneath, moves to its left and then up to the top. Before our flight, I explained in detail how to best execute the maneuver. Then we took off. At 1,000 feet about three miles west of Henley, I said, "OK, Dick, box-the-wake."

Passengers Marj Denniston and Sharon Bulloch following glider flight with Gladys.

He reached up and pulled the tow release. "What now?" he asked. Caught off guard, it took me several seconds to react. "How could a commercial pilot do such a crazy thing?" I thought. "He must not have listened to a word I said!"

"Head for the airport," I told Dick through clenched teeth. "If we can't make it, I'll decide where to land." We did make it, only because we hit a small thermal that lifted us enough for the down-wind landing.

Although I walked away from that experience shaking my head, my most harrowing glider experience was still to come. I was flying passengers in the two-place Schweitzer 2-33 a number of years later when an airline captain and his son walked into the flight office inquiring about a glider ride. Since I could take only one at a time in the 2-33, I took out the son, then the captain. As the Piper Pawnee towed us west following take-off, I noticed a stormfront of rolling dust much like coastal fog rolling in from the ocean. I was concerned but figured I could land before the storm hit. Releasing from the tow plane at 2,500 feet, I knew instantly it was too late.

The wind threw us up like a leaf in a storm while 40 to 50 mph gusts, blew the tow plane off the runway, unable to land. Applying full dive brakes, I could see I had only one option. "The glider can't land on the runway with that crosswind," I told the captain. Instead I'd make my approach between the flight office and the cafe to gain the width of the tarmac and the width of the runway to land.

"You can't do that!" the Captain told me, visibly stressed. "Look at the trees!" Trees did indeed parallel the west side of the runway which I'm sure looked like a postage stamp from his front seat vantage point

"Don't worry," I told him. "Gliders don't need much room." What I didn't tell him was that I really had no other choice. To his credit, he said nothing more but grabbed the tubing on both sides as if to brace himself.

When the ground crew figured out my plan, pilots and

onlookers familiar with high wind procedures lined both sides of the tarmac to grab the glider once it touched the ground. The crosswinds rocked the glider madly as we headed in, but once we set down with the help of many hands, we didn't move more than ten feet. Without the ground crew's help, though, we would have been tumbled around like a paper airplane.

Once down, the captain was all smiles. "You did a superb job," he said. "It's hard to believe you could land in such a short distance." An hour later, he was still telling customers in the cafe about his ride.

By the early eighties, several years later, Henley's fleet of rental gliders and trainers drew glider pilots and students from a

Gladys removing Steven Hurley's shirt-tail following his solo in Schweitzer 2-33 - June 25, 1983.

50-mile radius or more. The FAA had insufficient help to flight test the glider students we were graduating. Fortunately, I had more glider experience than other pilots in the area and also met the requirements for an FAA Examiner, so the fall of 1983, Robert Hill, chief inspector of the FAA office in Spokane, came to Henley for a chat.

"Gladys," he said, "you know we need a glider examiner out here. You have the qualifications for a Private and Commercial glider examiner. All you need is to go to Oklahoma City for standardization training. We'll pay for your trip and training."

I had been appointed an airplane examiner for the CAA (Civil Aeronautics Authority) in 1944 for Private and Commercial, both land and sea, but the change from the CAA to FAA and also many changes in training regulations required that I take the schooling. I hedged long enough that Mr. Hill agreed I could set my own test fees and the FAA would supply my materials.

I enjoyed the trip and the training, but like most students, I wasn't exactly anxious to take the test. When I returned, I had plenty of students to test. For the examiner, it's critical to gauge how well a pilot reacts when something unexpected occurs. It kept me on my toes trying to think of new things for each applicant, like releasing the glider unexpectedly, keeping the dive brakes from releasing if the pilot needed to use them, holding the dive brakes so they wouldn't retract when needed, and many more. In 1985, Flight Instructor was added to my examiner's designation.

This all was yet to come, though. In early 1977 when Clay died, I was sixty two, not quite ready to retire, and worried about the Aerodrome's fate. I expected things to change, but little did I know the next few years would open an exciting new chapter in my life.

Chapter 21:
The Aerodrome's Demise

Clay's passing seemed to suck the life from Henley Aerodrome. We "Henleyites" went through the motions, with Joe Watts and I instructing and Clay's wife, Nadine, operating the Wing Over Cafe. Maybe we knew that time would bring change.

Until Clay's death, Joe and I had counted on Clay's Cubs for trainers. Afterwards we never knew from one day to the next if one would be available. Tired of the hassle, Joe eventually bought an Aeronca Champ and told me he'd pay me for the hours I flew. "You've got a DEAL," I said. Because I also had students almost ready for Private Pilot Certificates and required a plane with radio and adequate instruments for instrument training, I ran into problems again trying to schedule Clay's Cessna. My son-in-law, Dick (also an instructor) and I, along with two students, bought a Cessna 150, getting us by for a couple of years until a young entrepreneur introduced us to a new era for Henley Aerodrome

The change-artist was not a professional aviator. In fact his background would not have predicted what was to come. Gary Norton made his fortune building International Systems Corporation which manufactures data entry terminals for the financial industry. He began as the proverbial whiz kid, plowing through a two-year computer programming course at Florida's

Henley Aerodrome flight line - 1982.

Miami-Dade Community College in one semester, graduating immediately to the computer staff.

After working for several computer firms which landed him in Spokane, Gary decided to build a data entry system that Fidelity Mutual had requested but the computer supplier for whom Gary worked could not provide. And Gary did it—on his kitchen table! As one admirer put it, "That computer could do everything a bank teller could—but steal."

Demand for his system created a phenomenal market, and Gary met all his delivery deadlines, building his own company and amassing a fortune in the process. But running the business soon grew old. "When I've done everything there is to do at least once," Norton told a reporter, "I get bored." It wasn't long before he bailed out and began looking for a new challenge.

The summer following Clay's death, Norton neatly landed his airplane at Henley and taxied to Walt Redfern's workshop. Local air buffs recognized Norton as an ace pilot who used the field frequently, but no one knew him well. Gary found Walt at work on his latest replica and after admiring Walt's handiwork let it drop that he'd sure like to buy the place and carry on Clay's dream. "Why don't you go talk to Mrs. Henley at the Wing Over," Walt suggested. "I think it's for sale." Had Gary known what the next year would bring, he might have thought twice.

With little fanfare, Norton purchased Henley Aerodrome, Clay's Cessna 150, Joe's Travel Air and Aerona Champ, and a hangar (Joe had left for Alaska to fly the bush). To my relief I was able to continue flight training for Norton without a hitch.

Meanwhile Gary turned his creative genius toward developing Norton Aero Limited, Corporation. Although a few local skeptics didn't think a computer-nerd could run an operation like Henley, they soon found Gary could do darned near anything. His first project was to update the property. After purchasing land south of the runway, he bulldozed the old runway and fueling area, resurfaced the tarmac, taxiway and runway (which he extended to 4200 feet) and buried power lines on the runway's south end. Then he put in two 12,000 gallon fuel tanks.

His next priority was to line up staff. Gary's brother, Wayne Norton, was a skilled pilot who had just completed an aircraft and powerplant mechanics course and had also earned his A & P Certificate which qualified him to work on aircraft. Gary hired Wayne as manager of flight operations.

Meanwhile, I had retired from Kootenai Memorial Hospital in May 1980 and was left with some time on my hands. I'll never forget feeling free as a breeze as I drove home from my retirement party—no obligations, no financial worries, only blue skies ahead. During the next month, though, I discovered after flying and teaching all I wanted, along with flying passengers in the Travel Air 4000 for Gary on weekends, that I still had empty weekdays.

By this time Gary had hired Walt Redfern to build WW I replicas for the aerodrome's museum. It didn't take Walt long to sense I was itching for work. "Gladys, if you'd like to help, how about covering the Fokker Triplane I'm building."

"Okay," I said, thankful he'd made the suggestion. "But I warn you-it's been a few years since I've worked with fabric." I guess I needn't have worried. Ceconite, the synthetic material Walt used, turned out much easier to handle than the cotton Herb and I worked with in 1933. Over the next months, Walt's wife, Velda, and I covered a Sopwith Camel, Pitcairn Mail Wing, and an Albatross, to name a few

Before long the Aerodrome's plane squadron had grown to thirty, with antiques or warbirds accounting for about half. Included in Norton's collection were a Stinson Tri-motor; a 1926 American Eagle Biplane, featuring a unique water-cooled, V-8 engine; a 1928 Pitcairn Mail Plane; a 1930 Travel Air 4000 Biplane; and a 1932 Fleet Biplane. WW I replicas included a British SE5, a French Neiuport, a German Fokker Dr-I Triplane and a German Eindeker Monoplane. All flew or were being readied to fly and were eagerly awaited by an impatient public.

Norton announced Henley's first big air show would be July 28,1981. Word must have spread quickly as 2,500 spectators and

Gladys working on Albatros
aileron.

Gladys covering wing of
Albatros.

Albatros built by Bob Sleep and Walt Redfern at Silverwood - 1991. Now in
museum in Alabama.

more than five dozen aircraft from the Northwest and Canada converged on the aerodrome. Even a sprinkling of rain didn't dampen spectators' enthusiasm, many of whom took to the air themselves in biplanes and gliders or hopped on the 1931 Stinson Tri-motor. This eleven-passenger plane, the only operational one in the world, recalled an era of adventure.

By twilight I was exhausted, having flown dozens of passengers in the open cockpit Travel Air. When I finally made it to bed, I fell asleep immediately, only to be startled awake a few hours later. "What's wrong?" I asked myself. Groggy for a minute, I finally focused my eyes on shadows dancing wildly across the bedroom wall, then turned over to see lights flickering through the window. Good heavens! The Aerodrome hangar was lit up like a giant torch.

Dressing frantically, I soon joined the small crowd already gathered near the fire. Helpless, we watched as six hundred and fifty thousand dollars in vintage airplanes burned, none of them insured. Word traveled fast, and plane lovers started arriving at daybreak as if to mourn a friend's death. By sunset volunteers had hauled off and buried the debris. Norton estimated his loss at $1 million, including his newly purchased P51 Mustang WW II fighter. A metal plaque, cut from a puddle of aluminum found where it had been parked, is the only evidence of Henley's first collection of historic aircraft.

Gary took his lumps and began rebuilding his vintage squadron the winter of '82, unprepared for the next tragedy. On a brisk January morning, Gary's brother cleaned up the new stunt plane, a Pitts Special, for Gary to fly a little later. Since Wayne planned to participate in an air show the next day, he took the Pitts up to practice aerobatics—a free air show for lucky visitors hanging out at the Wingover. Things went fine until the plane dropped into a flat spin at which point, according to one spectator, "He just vanished behind the trees and never came back up." The Pitts had crashed, killing Wayne instantly.

In aviation news travels fast. I learned of Wayne's death in my hospital bed, where I was recovering from a cholecystectomy (removal of my gall bladder). Discharged the following day, I got home shortly before Wayne's father, Tom, came by the house. "Gladys," he said, "will you fly with me on Wayne's Memorial Flight?" Still weak and very sore from surgery, I couldn't imagine how I could help until it dawned on me he just wanted company.

"I'd be honored," I replied." The missing man formation originated during WW I when a comrade got killed. The remaining pilots would fly over their base, leaving a vacant space in the formation where their comrade had flown. This was to be our farewell to Wayne.

Gary took Wayne's death hard, but he still had an airport to run. "I need new manager," he told Walt a few days later. "You know anyone could do the job?"

Walt rubbed his chin for a moment. "Well, you know that Gladys taught during the war and ran a flight school afterwards. You couldn't find anyone better qualified."

"I know, Walt," Gary replied. "but she just retired."

"She retired to do more flying. Why don't you two talk?"

Gary dropped by the house that same day and just laid it on the line.

"I'm looking for someone to manage the Aerodrome. Walt thought you might be interested." I studied Gary's young, intelligent face for a minute. How well would we get along, I wondered, with me pushing seventy.

"Well, I've invested a lot in this place over the years," I replied after a bit. "I'm certainly interested in its success."

Gary suggested I think his proposal over and get back to him as soon as possible. When he left, I told myself immediately I'd enjoy the challenge but decided to sit on it a while to get used to the idea. A few days later we talked specifics. "What exactly will you expect me to do?" I asked. His answer was long—and a little scary.

"You'll handle operation, maintenance and safety of all aircraft used for flight school, training, passenger flights, charter and rentals. I also want you to hire dependable personnel to handle flight and maintenance. It'll be up to you to purchase any material and equipment we need to maintain the flight operation."

"Is that all?" I asked with a straight face.

He laughed and added, "I've insured everything, Gladys, and contracted out the Wingover Cafe. The flight operation will have to carry its own weight financially." We agreed on terms, and I started work the next day.

My first task was to line up personnel. After doing some figuring, I realized it would be more cost efficient to hire aircraft maintenance mechanics as needed rather than on a full time basis so worked out a deal with A & P Mechanics, Vic and Claudia Gendron at Hackney Air Park, who had formerly operated the Henley shop. Young Matt Hutchings, the existing lineman, wanted to stay on. He would service all the aircraft and take care of transit planes. With flight instructor, Mark Sweeney, and I teaching, everything seemed in place.

Once Gary determined I had taken control, he backed off and eventually moved to Arlington, Washington, where he built hangars to house his aircraft collection. Before he left he posted a "For Sale" sign at Henley. Three busy years passed while I managed the Aerodrome, its future hanging in the balance. Then one day Gary walked into Harrah's Museum Auction in Reno, Nevada, intending to look at a 1928 Ford Tri-Motor when he spied an old narrow-gauge locomotive. He and his wife looked at each other and said, "Why not?" That day Gary bought the Tri-Motor (the most money ever paid for an antique airplane), three automobiles (1916 Franklin, 1929 Model A Ford Cabriolet, and 1929 Model Station wagon), and he outbid Disneyland for the 1915 Porter steam engine and three miles of track.

Gary liked to take gambles, and gamble he did that day. At first he just planned to lay the train track, add a restaurant and store at Henley and let North Idaho folks enjoy the ride. Instead, what evolved over the next few years was **Silverwood**, Gary's re-creation of a mining town settled in the 1880's. Visitors could stroll down main street visiting a general store, saloon, train station, 100-seat restaurant, theater, and a 20,000 square foot museum of transportation, all serviced by a three-mile narrow gauge railroad. They could sit on the grass or in bleachers to watch Captain Eddie's Flying Circus, an action packed air show. Since Silverwood opened in 1989, Gary has added a variety of amusement rides and activities, all of which offer safe, clean entertainment for families at reasonable prices.

These changes saddened many Northwest pilots who preferred Henley over any other airport. Because of the new theme park, Gary downplayed the airport and discontinued flight instruction. Now, aircraft fuel is available only during the summer months when Silverwood is open. Even though a large grassy area invites transit aircraft to park, Henley's old camaraderie is gone.

For two years I managed the flight operation at Silverwood, flying gliders and on occasion the Pawnee tow plane and the Cessna 182 jump plane for the air show. By 1990 I moved into the flight office and chose to retire at the season's end.

Chapter 22: Retirement

One day I had a vision.
I dreamed that I could fly!
I chased my dream
down an old sunbeam,
and soon I sailed on high.

Long the path I met a star
to help me on my way.
Twas Gladys Buroker,
I know not what sparked her,
but I'm grateful to this day.

Back when the biplanes flew
was when her light awoke.
A girl of five...
          and much alive...
a subservient pattern soon broke.

She fell very much in love,
but not with mortal man.
An airplane flew over
a field of clover.
She ran to see it land.

From that day on her glow
so brilliantly poured forth.
She lit the skies,
to the world's surprise,
women's place moved up from the hearth.

(by former student)

The retirement years are a time for remembering, for pulling together the threads of one's life and weaving them into a single blanket. I ask myself, "Why did I make the choices that led to such an unconventional life?"

Part of the answer comes from my childhood which still seems so close. Can it really be 70 years since I pulled a sling shot from my dirty overalls and aimed a small, round rock at a robin behind our house, shattering its fragile wing? I'll never forget Mother's irritation over my tomboyish stunts. "I told you not to shoot at birds," she said, grabbing my arm. "Now you'll have to kill it."

"No! I can't," I yelled, struggling to get loose as tears ran down my cheeks. Finally, sensing the intensity of my distress, Grandma Dawson picked up the bird and wrung its tiny neck. Although we were never close, I was forever grateful to her, never shooting at another bird until Herb took me duck hunting.

At Christmas one year I asked mom for a pair of rubber boots, so I could play outside. If I wasn't roaming the woods, I was searching for scrap material to use in designing and building gadgets. When that magical moment arrived on Christmas morning and I ripped open my package, all I found was a frilly, yellow dress of

Gladys with sling shot, age 10.

244

satin...girl's stuff. Disappointment floated in the air that day, mine because I didn't get boots and Mother's because she stayed up late many nights sewing a gift I despised. I realized early on I was different from other little girls and rejected much of what my parents expected—especially my dad.

Could it be seven decades since Dad worked us kids so hard in his poultry business, sometimes making us dress fifty fryers at a time for company picnics? On slaughter days, he would hang the panicked birds by the feet to the clothes line, slit their throats, dip them in scalding water, and toss them still twitching into a washtub for us to pluck. I still remember the piles of feathers, the stink, the exhaustion.

It seems like yesterday that I walked up to a pilot at Tulip Field and said, "Excuse me mister. How much for a ride in that airplane?" I remember he looked me over carefully, no doubt surprised by my scruffy boys' overalls. When I pushed my hard-earned two dollars into his hand, though, he said, "Okay, climb aboard."

Moments later we flew thousands of feet above the earth. When I reached out my hand, I felt the rush of air. When I pulled it in, I felt nearly motionless. Straining against the seat harness, I spotted my high school and Old Settlers Park, looking like scale models I had seen at the county fair. I had no idea the Nooksack River twisted like a branch, that roads narrowed to trails, and cows looked like bugs.

When the pilot prepared to land, I held my breath, sure the engine would die. The ground came up fast...power lines ahead. All too soon we rolled to a stop. Ten minutes of seeing the world anew that day changed my life forever. At 16 I decided, in spite of my father, that I must fly again.

Now, at 83, I feel grateful for the road I've traveled. My boyishness, the difficult relationship I had with Dad, the freedom and beauty of flying launched me into a life few women dared attempt. While ignoring other's expectations, I barnstormed the Pacific Northwest and taught hundreds to fly. During the Thirties when women were baking brownies, starching shirts and gossiping at the beauty parlor, I went wing walking and learned to skydive. Accepted as one of the boys, I worked and played in their domain, yet still married and raised a family.

It shouldn't surprise anyone, then, that retirement doesn't suit me. In fact, it didn't stick the first time (when I left nursing), so I had to retire again (when I quit Silverwood). Hard work makes me feel healthy and alive. Maybe that's why I've taken on the many projects that fill my time since Silverwood. One major undertaking that ended only recently was the 20 year project of landscaping and maintaining my Henley property after I turned 60. I began by trimming trees and cutting dead wood for my fireplace, wearing out several chain saws in the process. After building a hangar below the house, I planted grass to the runway, so I could taxi out to fly whenever the mood struck me.

Wanting more than Lodge Pole and Bull Pine, I planted about 150 young trees—mostly Tamarack (Larch), Cedar, Blue Spruce, White Pine, Red and White Fir. Being an avid gardener, I also put in a garden and fruit trees. Disaster struck the first year as the elk and deer ate the tree limbs, the grouse ate the leaves and buds, and the pocket gophers ate the roots. As the fruit trees died, I replaced them with dwarf trees planted in buried boxes of half-inch hardware cloth, which protected the larger roots from the marauders. To fend off the deer I circled seven-foot metal fence posts, four to a tree, with wire, and to keep out the grouse I put netting over the top.

Although I recently moved to a new home in the woods near Rathdrum, ID, I still enjoy the company of wildlife in my yard. My companions are mostly flying buddies. There have been several gentlemen whose company I've enjoyed these past nineteen years, but marriage has been out of the question. No one could ever fill Herb's shoes. Instead I spend time with my three generations of offspring—children/ grandchildren/great-grandchildren— and a group of friends who still meet for Sunday morning breakfast at the Grey Goose in Athol. A week seldom passes without a former student or friend dropping by to ask questions and share hangar stories. These visits leave me feeling good for days.

Keeping busy every day has never been a problem, once the hurt of Herb's death diminished. While still at Henley, I turned my basement into a workshop. One year I built 32 bluebird houses to the specifications of the Idaho Game Department and placed them at Silverwood Theme Park, Silverwood RV Park, and on my place. Until I moved to Rathdrum, I cleaned and repaired them every fall. Before I started this book, I was building a radio-controlled airplane I hope to soon finish and fly. My latest project is building wing ribs for home-built replicas of vintage airplanes.

The only thing holding me back since retirement has been an obstacle that plagues most people my age—my health.

I've had a number of surgeries, the most frustrating of which has been on my right knee. I suspected in 1933, when I landed hard on a parachute jump for Jim Galvin, that my damaged right leg would haunt me for years to come—and it has. After a less-than-successful surgery in 1937, I wore a knee brace for several years and an elastic bandage off and on all my life. But it wasn't until I started nursing in 1967 that I noticed standing and heavy lifting seemed to bother my right hip and knee in particular. By 1986, I found getting into the Travel Air difficult and then noticed one day from my footprints in the snow that I walked with my right foot turned out. In March 1991, after I tolerated five years of pain in my right hip and knee, I decided to have hip replacement. My recovery went so well I asked to be scheduled for a knee replacement eight months later. Recovery this time did not come easily. After nine months of physical therapy and three years of consistent exercise, I still walk with a bad limp and need a cane. Even so, I resumed flying April 1992 but no longer fly commercially, instead donating my time to instructing and taking people for rides in my Cessna 172.

In spite of these frustrations, I've never lost the sense of humor that Herb and I shared. I think it's what keeps me going in hard times. About three months following my knee surgery, I was given a follow-up appointment for the first of April. On my way home I thought, "Gee, that gives me a month to figure out an April fool's joke." When I told my friends, they were skeptical. "You wouldn't do that to a doctor, would you?" I told my physical therapist that week that I needed to borrow a knee brace or support as part of the gag. "I've got just the ticket," Lee said, "a knee support football players use."

By the day of my appointment, I had already resumed walking with a cane, but instead I wore the knee support and hobbled in on crutches. When the nurse called me, I told him, "I have to see the doctor before any X-rays."

"What happened?" he asked.

"I can't talk about it," I replied. I knew when Dr. Brunjes walked in the nurse had told him something was wrong. "Are you in a lot of pain?" he asked.

"Yes," I said, "Nothing's helped."

"What happened?"

"I'm ashamed to tell you."

He pulled his stool closer to me and said gently, "You don't have to be ashamed."

I looked at him with sad eyes and began my yarn. "Yesterday was my birthday," I told him, "and my parachuting friends at Silverwood presented me with a ticket for a jump. I told them 'no thanks,' that I was on a cane and just couldn't. They coaxed and coaxed, saying they'd brought a buddy chute, so it wouldn't be any more difficult than stepping off a step"

By this time the doctor was shaking his head and scowling. "We had a beautiful jump," I continued. "Everything looked great until Danny hit a depression while landing, forcing me to take all the weight on my bad knee."

"Well, let's take a look," he said grimly. I reached down to undo the knee support, but the doctor said, "I want you up on a table." He and the nurse hauled me up, took off the support, and dropped their jaws at the sign I had made: APRIL FOOLS!

The nurse started laughing, but Dr. Brunjes just stared at the sign and finally looked up. "Is this a joke?" he asked

"Yeah," I answered with a little grin. This was the first time I'd ever seen the man at a loss for words.

"Take the X-rays," he told the nurse. "Then I'll check the knee." Without comment he walked from the room. Back a few minutes later, he kept saying, "I've never had anyone do anything like that before." He wasn't mad—just surprised.

Another of my favorite stories took place when Kelly and his family came to Henley one Sunday for dinner. After cleaning his plate, my grandson, Ben, went outside to play but ran back in again yelling, "There's a bear out here!" Kelly and I grabbed our cameras and headed for the door, only to find a young yearling black bear watching us about ten feet away.

Ben started his motor bike, startling the bear, which ran a little ways, then climbed about fifteen feet up a tree. My daughter-in-law, Marilyn, yelled, "Ben, come back; the mother bear will be close." Kelly and I both walked to the tree and snapped some pictures, while Marilyn begged us to return.

"It's too old, Marilyn," I said. "There won't be a sow around." I walked back to the doorway to reassure her while Kelly, still at the tree, urged her to join him. She took a few hesitant steps, then finally reached the tree, all the while looking for

Yearling black bear in Gladys' back yard at Henley Aerodrome.

249

the mother which she knew to be close by. That's when the devil made me do it.

"There's the mother," I yelled, at which she literally flew back to the house, through brush, her feet barely touching the ground. Everyone laughed except Marilyn. When I saw how frightened she was, I put my arm around her and said, "I'm sorry." I think she's forgiven me by now but only because she's such a sweetheart.

I think of one beautiful sight I've seen three times during my flying career. Encountering a condition that produces a 360 degree rainbow that circles the airplane like a halo. This rainbow moves along with the aircraft, like a guardian angel until the aircraft flies out of the existing meteorological condition. The rainbow is caused by an arch of light, formed opposite the sun, exhibiting the colors, causing refraction, reflection, and dispersion of light on water droplets. It is a truly beautiful experience. Many pilots have never encountered this phenomenon.

I learned early if I truly wanted to get something, I needed dedication and determination. I made plenty of mistakes, but I learned a lesson in the process. Going that extra mile for employers brought promotions, more responsibility and higher income.

A woman mustn't worry about others' opinions when she chooses an out-of-the-ordinary vocation. If she has the desire and does her job well, she'll be admired for taking on something that other women didn't have the guts to try. Much progress has been made in equal rights for women throughout the last fifty years, and if women continue doing what they want, I predict there will be equality in fifty more years.

I may be the luckiest woman alive, with my family, working at something I loved, and the recognition that's come to me over the past ten or fifteen years.

AWARDS AND RECOGNITIONS

1976   Featured flying a Tiger Moth vintage airplane in the promotional film for the movie THE AMELIA EARHART story.

1988   Featured on Public Television's "Northwest Profiles" program a Spokane affiliate of CBS.

1989   Presented Hall of Fame, Pathfinder Award by Jeff Renner of KING-TV at the Museum of Flight, Seattle, Washington.

1989   Presented with the 0X5 Pioneer Award in Wichita, Kansas

1990   Profile: The Life of Gladys Buroker, Pilot presentation in Edmonton, Alberta, Canada.

1991   Featured on Public Television special, "The Collectors" (military memorabilia).

1991   Presented Instructor of the Year Award by the N. W. Section of the Federal Aviation Administration, Tacoma, Washington.

1992   Museum of Oshkosh (Wisconsin) exhibit, The Life of Gladys Buroker.

1992   Presented with J.C. Penney Spirit of The American Woman Award in Coeur d'Alene, Idaho.

1992   Guest on "Aviation Talk", National Public Radio.

1993   Featured in educational video "The Young Astronauts" for use in classrooms.

1995   Presented, Idaho Aviation "Hall of Fame" Award, Boise, Idaho.

1995   Featured on Idaho Public Television "Flying Idaho Back Country".

1996   Featured, Building Wing Ribs for vintage aircraft, Spokane KXLY, an affiliate of ABC.

1996   Certificate of Recognition by Idaho Governor Phillip E. Batt for outstanding achievement, 19,605 hours of Aviation Safety.

1996   Presented 0X5 Hall of Fame Award, Seattle, Washington.